BROKEN AMERICA

TEN GUIDING PRINCIPLES
TO RESTORE AMERICA

---

by

JIM WHITE, PHD

JLW

Inspiring Excellence
in People

JL White International, LLC
16220 N. Scottsdale Road, Suite 260
Scottsdale, AZ 85254

Note: *This publication is presented solely for informational, educational, and entertainment purposes. It is not intended to provide legal, financial, political, or investment advice and should not be relied upon as such. If expert assistance is required, the services of a professional should be sought. The publisher and the author and their affiliated entities and individuals do not make any guarantees or other promises as to any results that may be obtained from using the content of this book. To the maximum extent permitted by law, the publisher and the author and their affiliated entities and individuals disclaim any and all liability in the event any information contained in this book proves to be inaccurate, incomplete, or unreliable, or results in any investment or other losses. Further, the laws and regulations referenced in this book may vary from state-to-state and are subject to change. You, the reader, are responsible for your own choices, actions, and results.*

978-0-9795216-8-3 Ebook ISBN
978-0-9795216-7-6 Print book ISBN
Printed in the United States of America

Dear America,

This book is dedicated to you.

I ask for your indulgence and open mind as you read these pages. Some of my words may sting and some may disappoint.

My greatest desire is that these ten principles—whether you agree with every example or not—will inspire you to stand up for our great nation. She has provided us with endless opportunities and, in my opinion, is in jeopardy. She is in pain. She is asking for all patriots to protect her.

Please heed her call before it's too late.

JLW

We in America do not have government by the majority. We have government by the majority who participate.

~Thomas Jefferson, 3rd President of the United States

Great principles don't get lost once they come to light; they're right here! You just have to see them again.

~Jefferson Smith (portrayed by James Stewart),
Mr. Smith Goes to Washington

Acknowledgments

I cannot express enough thanks to my publishing team for their continued support and encouragement: Gary M. Krebs, Amy Cooper, Deborah Levison, Lily Nixon, and Libby Kingsbury.

The completion of this book could not have been accomplished without the support of the many great Americans who inspire me on a daily basis.

Finally, to my caring, loving, and supportive wife: my deepest gratitude. Your encouragement when the times got rough are duly noted and much appreciated. It was a great comfort and relief to know that you were willing to provide management of our life activities while I completed my work. My heartfelt thanks.

And to my two sons, Taylor and Myles: Thank you for your inspiration and support.

Table of Contents

JULY 4, 1776.

We the People

ensure domestic Tranquility, provide for the common defence,
and our Posterity, Wordain and establish this Constitution

Article I

Preface

A CALL TO ACTION FOR SUSTAINING AMERICA'S FUTURE

Learn to think continentally.

~Alexander Hamilton, 1ˢᵗ United States Secretary of Treasury

This is not a book written exclusively for Democrats. Or Republicans. Or Liberals. Or Conservatives. Or Tea Party members. Or Independents. Or Libertarians. Or those who have so-called Socialist views. Or people who belong to lesser-known or extinct parties. (Are there any Tories and Whigs still out there?) Or even individuals who have no political affiliations whatsoever.

This book is for the above—*all Americans*. I don't care one iota about which party you belong to (or none at all); where your family originated from; your religious beliefs; the color of skin; if you live in an urban or rural area; if your earnings fall into the low, middle, or high economic range; or if you root for the Boston Red Sox or the New York Yankees baseball team (or don't like baseball at all).

If you are an American, this book is for you.

By virtue of our Constitution and its Amendments, all Americans are equal. We have the luxury of immense personal freedom and liberty. We have a right to believe whatever we want and to publicly express our views. No matter what our differences might be, we (all Americans, that is) agree on one thing: *love for our country*.

Finding common ground to unite all Americans is one of the main themes of this book, and it is my sincere hope that you will fully embrace this concept. You only need to come to the table with three pre-requisites: a love of our country, an open heart, and an open mind.

I realize that the ideas I am about to present in this book may at first seem agenda driven. I assure you that they aren't. We are all a bit jaded in this day-and-age and, perhaps rightly, have become skeptical of anyone who writes any kind of politically themed treatise.

Please bear with me as I earn your trust regarding the above. I also ask that you understand why I am so passionate about this subject—so much so, in fact, that I allowed its creation to take a significant part of my mindshare away from pressing business ventures and other book projects.

WHAT IS *BROKEN AMERICA*?

The title of this book is intentionally provocative. My goal is, of course, to capture your attention right away about the dire situation of our nation. Put simply, *Broken America* is a call to action for all Americans to put political party aside and unite under our country's founding principles.

It's perfectly all right for us to disagree and debate about the issues we face. However, the disputes have become so ugly and predictably partisan that the very fabric of our nation has become frayed and the flag is being torn apart at the seams.

Reuniting the United States of America under common principles may strike you as a naïve, utopian endeavor. Or, perhaps you believe it is presumptuous of me to assume that this is *the next big thing* that should happen in our nation.

Before embarking on this project, I arrived at the conclusion that I had to do *something* about America's continuing political crisis. I became convinced that the high stakes warrant immediate action. Our way of life depends on it.

I answered this call to action. Will you be brave enough to rise up and do the same? If enough people act, my reunited vision of America behind these ten guiding principles will no longer be a pipe dream. It will become reality.

A FEW SIMPLE GROUND RULES

Below I have outlined a few basic ground rules in order to establish and maintain a universal understanding among all readers. They should not cause anyone to recoil. If you happen to disagree with any of them, that's fine. You are entitled to your own opinion; as I already mentioned, this is a free country. When you write your book, you are at liberty to create whatever ground rules you like.

1. **The Truth Matters**: We should never argue indisputable facts. I don't care what party you belong to or which media source you follow. Facts are facts; the truth is golden.

2. **Proven Scientific Principles Are Facts:** Scientists debate things all of the time and perspectives sometimes change based on the latest research, technology, and discoveries. But if, say, 99% of legitimate present-day scientists and medical authorities concur that a certain theory has been proven or an epidemic requires social distancing, we are going to count it as fact. I happen to have a PhD, but I don't make any pretense that my degree is in science or that I know more about physics, geology, or medicine than a Nobel Prize winner, university professor, or M.D. in those areas. I would never have attempted to argue with Einstein (assuming he were still alive) about the Theory of Relativity,

would you? If you didn't study the sciences, trust the scientists.

3. **Politicians Often Lie:** Some might even go as far as saying politicians are *paid* to lie. I'm not suggesting that all politicians lie all of the time; some do so a lot more than others and to varying degrees. But we must always hold them accountable for telling the truth. Part of a journalist's role is to probe and question in search of the truth, which should be encouraged; often they expose lies, which is one of the things that distinguishes us from dictatorships, banana republics, and other forms of government that control the media.

4. **Political Propaganda About Fake News Is Often *Genuine Fake News* Itself:** This harkens back to #3, Politicians Lie. When politicians refer to something as fake news, they may be doing so because they have seen a headline they don't like or agree with—probably because it casts them in a negative light. Be mindful, however, that there is indeed a lot of hooey out there intended to harm politicians and their families. Let's agree to stop going down the road of spreading such trash.

5. **Russia Attacked Our 2016 Elections:** This is another proven fact. All of our intelligence agencies and the Mueller Investigation have confirmed that Russia hacked our elections (through bots on social media, for example) in order to disrupt our Democracy. It worked in the sense that it caused even more friction

among us. I will not suggest that Donald Trump did not win the 2016 Presidency or that his victory was illegitimate. Rather, that we agree election meddling is continuing to be a major threat to our country and we must be vigilant against it ever happening again in the future. Ponder this: Even if the result favors your candidate and party, do you really wish to side with Vladimir Putin and Russia—our enemy—over our own Democracy and fellow patriots?

6. **What's Right for Our Country Overrules Political Party:** Whether you are a Democrat or Republican, the United States of America always comes first. We Pledge Allegiance to our nation, not to a President or any kind of political agenda. Let's agree to stop thinking of our personal political party as we would a beloved sports team. Whereas a sports fan is rarely going to agree with an umpire's call that favors the other team, we must do so when it comes to what is best for our country. We need to yank off our political jerseys and rally caps when it comes to upholding our nation's principles. (We'll spend a lot more time on this in the Introduction.)

Now that you know the intended audience for this book, understand why I have written it, and have acknowledged my call to action and this book's six simple ground rules, please join me as we pinpoint where our nation has gone off-course and how we may right it.

Introduction

LET'S RIGHT THE COURSE
OF OUR NATION

A great empire, like a great cake,
is diminished at its edges.

~Benjamin Franklin, statesman, writer, inventor

RED, WHITE, AND BLUE

We love these colors—they conjure up thoughts of freedom, patriotism, our states, and our beautiful flag. Break
these colors apart and what do you have? A fractured country perilously divided by red and blue.

The concept of parties representing groups of people who share specific political ideas dates all of the way
back in American history to 1787 and the infamous battles between the Federalists (led by Secretary of Treasury
Alexander Hamilton) and the Anti-Federalists (headed by
Secretary of State Thomas Jefferson). If you happen to be
a fan of Broadway theater and can afford the steep price
of admission, you will learn all about this massive colonial ideological clash (and others) in the smash-hit musical
Hamilton. This entertaining and educational show proves
the adage that great minds don't always think alike.

RED, WHITE, AND BLACK-AND-BLUE

Today's color-coated state divides are believed to have
begun in 1976 when NBC News anchor John Chancellor
announced that states won by Democrat Jimmy Carter
would be represented on a map in blue, while those won
by Republican incumbent Gerald Ford would be shown in

red. The map of the United States on the TV screen was likely intended as an eye-grabbing, immediate way of showing which candidate was in the lead—and how he arrived there. It goes without saying that this worked—so well, in fact, that party members on each side thereafter adopted their respective color with pride as a unifying element.

Rah-rah-rah—play ball! Ever since and forever onward, it's been the red team vs. the blue team. Either you wear your team's color and jersey to the game, or you aren't considered a "true fan."

Where else are colors a popular way to divide opposing sides? Each nation around the globe uses a different color scheme on their respective flags to encourage unity and patriotism. In some summer camps, "color war" breaks out with kids assigned to competing teams labeled by color. The game of chess—which is really a lightly veiled metaphor for a royal battle—separates black-and-white, while checkers essentially does the same but with red and black.

Is politics really a game or sport? By virtue of color association representing a political team, we are already presumed to believe in certain principles linked to that party. We become pressured to support the party, no matter what the cause or issue might be. We are cornered into thinking we must always remember which team we are on and serve as a constant cheerleader for it. The other team, by default, is the enemy and therefore must be defeated on every issue.

Hold on a minute there, coach. Our friends, relatives, neighbors, and coworkers likely don't all wear the same political jersey color. Does that mean we are now enemies?

Political color divisions split our country further apart every day. Heaven forbid if a Democrat ever votes red or a Republican votes blue; that voter is an evil traitor to the party!

I know someone who lives in an East Coast blue state and happens to be a low-key Democrat. He loves his country just as much as the next person and is proud of the American flag. Now, however, he admits genuine fear when he sees a pickup truck with a driver wearing a red hat and an American flag blowing beside the windshield. He can't help but believe this fellow is a racist and, possibly, a white supremacist. But is he right with this stereotype?

In the 2020 season premiere of the HBO comedy *Curb Your Enthusiasm*, the show's star Larry David (as himself, of course) wears a red "Make America Great" (MAGA) hat in order to avoid having to mingle with people he doesn't like. His tactic works with flying colors (as it were); no one in L.A. wants anything to do with him and flee at the sight of him under the hat. It's a hilarious satirical statement on our contemporary culture that something as simple as wearing a hat can invite such divisive reactions.

And yet…here we are. A nation locked in an evenly matched color war. When there is a disagreement between the Democrats and Republicans, most people automatically defer to their color—red or blue.

How can we ever right our nation's ship when the enmity on both sides is so powerful and pervasive? To bring up the sports reference again, it would be like asking a New York Yankees fan (navy blue and gray pinstripes) to root for the Boston Red Sox (bright red). Fans who are brave enough to wear their team's jersey to a game at the opponent's home stadium are frequently subjected to severe vocal—if not even physical—abuse.

Some people have been known to get downright hostile toward fans of other teams—and that's just when it comes to a simple baseball game! But is it okay to do the same to a fellow American who wears a different color political hat? Aren't we supposed to be on the *same team* (i.e., country)?

But let's not place all of the blame for the red state/blue state conundrum on the 1976 NBC News team and the myriad news channels that have followed suit since then. A great deal of the responsibility also resides within the political parties and the politicians themselves who continue to stoke the flames that partition our states and our country and pin us against ourselves.

When a politician is elected into office—I don't care if it's at the town, city, county, state, or national level—this individual automatically becomes a civil servant. What this means to me is that he or she represents *everyone*—red, blue, or purple. Yes, the leader is expected to fulfill campaign promises that happen to be party-driven; but, after that, the concerns and needs of the entire population must override the needs of the party. The people in charge must *do what is right* with upcoming votes in the next election be damned. Otherwise, you have a situation where the "losing team" gets buried into the ground—all so that a politician can get re-elected.

By way of example: We know there are specific government leaders who only wear neckties representing his political party. Red for Republican, blue for Democrats. Aren't all Americans of both parties paying millions in taxes that feed this individual's lifestyle and protect his family? Why would someone want to support a leader who makes it 100% clear from what he displays around his neck that he doesn't have your back?

I'm not suggesting for one second that anyone stop paying taxes. But I am proposing that leaders, once sworn into office, must set the example and forego the color jersey play entirely. This is when it's time to ditch the hats, the ties, and the other color-biased paraphernalia that excludes millions of American patriots. If you must wear a tie, try switching off between red and blue. Or don one that is patriotic red, white, and blue. Or, don't wear a tie at all. I don't think anyone cares so much about the tie so much anymore, anyway!

Symbols and colors are meaningful, whether obvious or subliminal. If athletes on both sides of a football game all wore the same colors, we wouldn't know which of them to root for or against. The same goes for politics—which is my point, exactly.

A MOMENT IN TIME—WHEN TEAMS AND FANS WERE POLITICALLY COLORBLIND

Back on September 11, 2001, the worst tragedy imaginable happened: America was attacked on several fronts by terrorists who hijacked several of our planes and weaponized them against us. The most vicious attacks came in the form of two commandeered airplanes ramming into each of the Twin Towers of the World Trade Center. Over 2,700 innocent lives were lost with thousands more injured, including many brave firefighters, officers, and others who went above and beyond to rescue victims.

At the time, the furthest thing on the minds of Americans was normalcy. Some of the thoughts racing through people's minds: *How do we go about our daily business after suffering so much pain and anguish? For Americans—especially New Yorkers—what is a reasonable mourning period? Are we even safe from additional attacks?*

In Queens, New York, subsequent to the horrific events, Shea Stadium—then the stadium of the New York Mets baseball team—became something of a central hub for firefighters, officers, volunteers, and others to recover from the rescue missions and strategize next steps. The last thing on anyone's mind on September 12 was assembling athletes on that field to "Play Ball!" Major League Baseball postponed its schedule for one week as they deliberated on how to handle the situation with sensitivity and respect. Some people felt it was too soon for America to enjoy itself with its pastime while the wounds were so fresh. Others believed sports could be a healing, unifying factor. This was uncharted territory for everyone concerned; there really was no right or wrong answer.

On Friday September 21, Major League Baseball decided the time had come to resume the schedule, and the first post 9/11 game took place at Shea Stadium with families of those lost, as well as dignitaries, firefighters, and New York's finest in attendance to watch the New York Mets play the Atlanta Braves. The pre-game ceremonies were solemn and touching. Tears were shed. The crowd burst into chants of "USA! USA! USA!" with waving flags and banners as if it were a heated moment during the Olympics taking place on American soil.

The game began and the proceedings settled back into the usual baseball rituals. It was just another regular game, right? But then things changed in the bottom of the eighth inning. Down by one run, Mets catcher Mike Piazza came to bat. The fans felt something in the air and the noise level rose. And then the impossible happened: The future Hall of Famer cracked a homerun and the Mets snatched the lead. The crowd erupted in a frenzy one might only experience if this had been the end of a World Series win.

But that was not all: Americans all over the country became joyous and positively giddy over Mike Piazza's victorious game winner. People from rural and urban communities all around our nation wholeheartedly embraced the spectacle of what had happened on the baseball diamond in Queens, New York.

Did Americans in Atlanta, Cleveland, Houston, Pittsburgh, Milwaukee, or Chicago care that Mike Piazza wasn't wearing the "right color" jersey? That question can only be answered with a resound *No*. They cheered because America was back! People didn't care which team you rooted for, what political party you belonged to, or which cap you wore. For one fleeting moment, the United Stated States of America was truly "united." All because of Mike Piazza's heroic swing.

How is it possible something as simple as the crack of a bat can bring such a diverse nation together—in spite of all of our differences? And yet, in the years since, we have sadly forgotten the lessons learned from the aftermath of 9/11 and have reverted back to rooting for our political team jerseys more than our country.

We are polarized to the extreme—and not even our shared love of America's pastime can bring us back from the brink.

WE ARE OFF-COURSE AND ADRIFT

The social issues we face in America are not new; racial intolerance, religious prejudice, economic imbalance, and ideological extremism have long existed in this country. Much of this seems to have been submerged, but it's always been lurking below the surface. Tragic events—such as the August 2017 Charlottesville car rampage, hate crimes committed on the campus of Syracuse University in November 2019, and the anti-Semitic stabbing at a rabbi's home in Monsey, New York in December 2019—have become all too frequent, as have incidents of mass-shootings in schools and public places.

Suddenly, the ugly radical underbelly of America has been unleashed. Americans are hurting fellow Americans far worse than our foreign enemies and, certainly, doing more damage to ourselves than any group of immigrants ever have.

Is anyone specifically to blame for this? Politicians? The

news media? Social media? Or, has the average American turned a blind eye to the polarization because he or she felt the need to overlook such things to help the chosen party win an election, line their pockets, or get certain legislation passed?

Painful as it may be, I believe it's time to cast aside all blame. We need bygones to be bygones. America is off-course and far adrift, which means the wounds are fresh and sore.

People rightly don't appreciate being called "deplorables." Or "libtard." Or any one of a million other slurs. The rhetoric is out of control on both sides, and it needs to stop. *Immediately.* We are at war with ourselves. While many people are convinced that suggestive political rhetoric is the cause of increasing violence, I do not think it is necessary to go there and state this outright at this time, whether true or not. Instead, I would like to suggest that childish name calling, cyber-bullying, and Twitter-venting only pours more salt into existing patriot vs. patriot wounds and divides us further apart, empowering and strengthening our true overseas enemies.

You are probably asking: How can we possibly all come to the table to negotiate and compromise on our serious political differences with all of these school playground squabbles continuing to happen every day?

I admit, it's easy to be offended. Politicians and media outlets *want* you to feel offended. These sentiments rile up emotions, such as anger and prejudice, and increase ratings and the number of attendees at political rallies.

Here is my rallying cry: It's time to cease and desist all of the childish name-calling and slurs and bring some level and decorum back into everyday politics. We must right this ship now or the extremist behavior is going to spiral out of control with no way of ever turning back.

Broken America is my way of rebooting our country through ten restorative principles intended to right our ship and bring us back on course. I don't care which party you belong to: Democrat, Republican, Liberal, Conservative, or anything in between, this book will hopefully resonate for you. At the very least, perhaps it will quell some of the heated political arguments that have occurred over festive meals during Easter, Passover, Thanksgiving, Christmas, Hanukah, and other celebratory family get-togethers.

It is not my intent to preach and sermonize, but if my language comes across as such in the chapters that follow, so be it. The stakes are too high for us to turn a blind eye and not do something about it. My ten principles—*Vision; Leadership; Truth-Seeking; Courage; Integrity; Tolerance and Equality; Respect; Patriotism; Capitalism and Money; and Compromise*—have all been meticulously selected for their simplicity, direct messaging, and universal characteristics. If you don't agree with any of them—well, I suggest you take some time and read and understand our Constitution. In fact, I believe the words and of our Founding Fathers are so relevant and important today that I've devoted the entire next part of this book to them.

To quote John Adams: "Always stand on principle...even if you stand alone."

PART ONE

The Wisdom of
Our Founding Fathers

> We have it in our power
> to begin the world again.
>
> —*Thomas Paine*

L et's do a roll call of our most significant America's Founding Fathers: *George Washington. Thomas Jefferson. John Adams. Samuel Adams. Benjamin Franklin. Alexander Hamilton. James Madison. Thomas Paine. John Hancock. John Jay. Patrick Henry. Paul Revere.*

We would be committing a grave injustice if we did not pay equal respect and attention to our Founding Mothers: *Abigail Adams. Martha Washington. Betsy Ross. Mercy Otis Warren. Molly Pitcher. Sybil Ludington. Phyllis Wheatley. Hannah Adams. Judith Sargent Murray. Elizabeth Schuyler Hamilton. Esther Reed. Dolley Madison. Deborah Sampson.*

Consider the remarkable good fortune for the fledgling colonies to have had over two dozen such extraordinary patriots alive at the same time, devoting their collective genius toward establishing the foundations of what would become the United States of America. Is it even possible to name an era and place in world history when so many accomplished people worked side-by-side to build a country?

At the very least, you would be hard-pressed to come up with a similar case study in modern history. You might have to go all of the way back to ancient Greece, Rome, or China to find such an assortment of brilliant, dedicated minds and, even then, few of those individuals played a simultaneous role in the creation of their respective governments.

Yes, America was truly blessed during colonial times. The leaders exemplified courage, big ideas, and high ideals. Don't get me wrong: They had plenty of disagreements and clashes and were far from perfect—Jefferson, in particular, had a dark side and was a slaveholder—but they were all bold, exceptional, unique individuals during a troubled time period.

Our first six Presidents—George Washington, John Adams, Thomas Jefferson, James Madison, James Monroe, and John Quincy Adams—all seem larger-than-life today. You don't, for example, hear anyone these days bashing George Washington because he was a Federalist.

Certainly, no one even thinks twice about the fact that Thomas Jefferson and James Madison organized what was then known as the Democrat-Republican party. (Can you believe it? Democrats and Republicans were once *one and the same*! Perhaps the elephant and donkey just need to give each other a hug every now and then….)

Centuries later, Americans are unable to agree upon contemporary Presidents whom everyone regards as even close to being mentioned in the same breath as the original six—mainly because of political party. Democrats would dismiss both Presidents named Bush. Republicans would knock off Presidents named Clinton and Obama. The only two names where at least some measure of positive consensus might be found? Reagan and Kennedy. Before then, possibly Truman and both Roosevelts—but that is already going pretty far back in history and, as it happens, primarily during war times when the country was unified against global enemies.

If we were to dive deeper into examining the successful modern political administrations, can we even begin to name more than one statesman or stateswoman who held office at the same time and reached the level of our achievement of our Founding Fathers and Mothers? No, because it simply hasn't happened.

This is precisely why I believe we must first look backward to the wisdom of the colonials in order for us to ever be able to successfully move forward.

WARRIORS, REBELS, MERCHANTS, CRAFTS-PEOPLE, PHILOSOPHERS, DIPLOMATS, WRITERS, AND MORE

The revolutionary era leaders were a diverse bunch, to say the least. George Washington was a surveyor who fought alongside the British during the French and Indian War. (It's also not commonly known that the first four Presidents—Washington, Adams, Jefferson, and Madison—initially considered themselves British subjects.) Benjamin Franklin was the closest America has ever had to a bona fide renaissance man: renowned inventor, writer, humorist, diplomat, and so much more. Betsy Ross ran an upholstery business. John Hancock was a merchant who resided in England to foster business contacts. Paul Revere was a silversmith and engraver. And on and on....

Some of our Founding Fathers and Mothers were well-educated, whereas others were not. Many started out with seemingly zero political leanings and then matured into seasoned politicians.

Eventually, the right group of the right people at the right time banded together and did the unthinkable: They made the bold decision to split from England—a far more powerful and established monarchy with a massive, well-trained military and naval fleet—and wage war against them. In 1776, Thomas Jefferson—assisted by a committee of five that included Benjamin Franklin and John Adams—penned the Declaration of Independence, a masterpiece memorializing the colonies' formal separation from the Mother Ship. Against all odds, the patriots defeated the opposition in the Revolutionary War, founding a whole new separate nation under the principles of Democracy. They created a unifying government structure, a series of binding laws, a functioning economic system and currency, a wealth of representational symbols, and a way of life based on life, liberty, and the pursuit of happiness. Amen!

Let's not ever forget that it was a group of warriors, rebels, merchants, craftspeople, philosophers, diplomats, writers, and more who built the finest democracy in the history of the world. And our victorious Continental Army consisted of volunteer soldiers—a large portion of whom were teenage farmers and hunters—hailing from all thirteen states, including numerous freed African American slaves, immigrants, and even some women dressed as men. Jewish Americans also made countless contributions to the Revolutionary War effort, including: suffering the first loss of a soldier (Francis Salvador); provisioning soldiers (Mordecai Sheftall of Savannah, GA); and financing the effort (Haym Solomon, who died broke as a result of his donations).

The next time anyone tells you that America must become great again by returning to something resembling a Confederate-like state, remind them that our colonial roots indicate this was the exact opposite of what our Founding Fathers and Mothers had in mind. Even more to the point: Given America's current diversity, immense body of knowledge, resources, and technological prowess, I am led to believe that we have a wealth of remarkable leaders among us today who may not be politicians *per se*—but are more than willing and capable of following the colonial legacy and righting the course of our democratic ship.

LET'S START AT THE TOP: OUR COMMANDER-IN-CHIEF

Once the British were defeated, the colonials had precious little time to set about the monumental task of founding a nation that would sustain itself. Only six brief years after the official end of the Revolutionary War, in 1789,

George Washington—the Commander-in-Chief of the Continental Army—was elected the first President of the United States...*unanimously*! Can you remotely imagine this circumstance occurring today?

It is widely known that George Washington didn't even *desire* to become President; if he'd had his druthers, he would not have hesitated to instead retire for the simple life with his beloved wife, Martha, in Mt. Vernon, New York. His non-controversial campaign slogan, "American Fabius," was a nickname he earned during the Revolutionary War because he had based some of his military strategy upon those of a Roman leader bearing that name. Picture seeing "American Fabius" on a political bumper sticker or baseball cap today!

President Washington accomplished many things while in office, beginning with, well, establishing the office for every President who followed after him. Recognizing the country needed settling down, he kept America neutral from the war between France and England; established the United States Navy; and, for his final finish, delivered what is perhaps the greatest Farewell Address of any President in our history. Interestingly, the famous speech was drafted by several brilliant minds, including James Madison and Alexander Hamilton.

Those who are even the slightest bit skeptical about the lasting wisdom of President Washington and his relevance today should pay close attention to the words in his Farewell Address:

> *The alternate domination of one faction over another, sharpened by the spirit of revenge, natural to party dissension, which in different ages and countries has perpetrated the most horrid enormities, is itself a frightful despotism. But this leads at length to a more formal and*

permanent despotism. The disorders and miseries, which result, gradually incline the minds of men to seek security and repose in the absolute power of an individual; and sooner or later the chief of some prevailing faction, more able or more fortunate than his competitors, turns this disposition to the purposes of his own elevation, on the ruins of Public Liberty.

One faction over another…party dissention…this leads at length to a more formal and permanent despotism…

Sound familiar? President George Washington and his speech writers foreshadowed our exact political climate today all of the way back in 1789.

The speech continues:

It is of infinite moment, that you should properly estimate the immense value of your national Union to your collective and individual happiness…and indignantly frowning upon the first dawning of every attempt to alienate any portion of our country from the rest, or to enfeeble the sacred ties which now link together the various parts.

In other words, America must be *united*. Its leaders must be inclusive, not exclusive, of fellow countrymen and women—even when we disagree. If we do—especially with regard to politics—our nation as a whole will fracture and weaken.

I admit that tears well up in my eyes as I read this next passage:

The name of American, which belongs to you in your national capacity, must always exalt the just pride of patriotism more than any appellation derived from local discriminations. With slight shades of difference, you have the same religion, manners, habits, and political principles. You have in a common cause fought and triumphed together; the independence and liberty you possess are the work of joint counsels, and joint efforts of common dangers, sufferings, and successes.

I urge all of us to heed the above prophetic and profound words of the Father of Our Country. Instead of attacking people who don't share the same worldview and/or politics, let's save all of our vitriolic rhetoric and nasty social media posts for our true enemies and national threats (i.e., terrorists, representing an obvious one).

WHY IS THE UNITED STATES CONSTITUTION SO RELEVANT TODAY?

The Constitution—initially something of a do-over to replace the flawed Articles of Confederation—was written during the Constitutional Convention in Philadelphia between May 25, 1787 and September 27, 1787, the day on which it was officially signed. The "Father" of the document was James Madison. The term "author" would be a stretch. During the four months of its deliberation, many colonial leaders—including Madison, Washington, Hamilton, and Franklin—had significant input on the final document. The path toward ratification was not an easy one behind closed doors. Back then, it was the Federalists (pro-Constitution) vs. the anti-Federalists (anti-Constitution). You may be surprised to learn that a certain patriot named Patrick Henry was in the latter camp.

Of course, our framers ultimately brought the document to closure, and it was accepted as the law of the land. Benjamin Franklin, who always had a quip at the tip of his tongue, famously remarked: "Our new Constitution is now established, everything seems to promise it will be durable; but, in this world, nothing is certain except death and taxes."

Thought it has frequently been tested, the Constitution has indeed proven to be durable and has nobly withstood the test of time.

Why is the Constitution of the United States still regarded as our country's most valuable document? Why should it continue to be viewed as sacred? (Note: I don't mean to in any way suggest that it's at the same level as holy religious texts, such as the Bible, the Torah, the Koran, etc.)

The answer is simple: Without it, we would be independent, conflicted states where people live in constant fear from our neighbors and/or the government, and we would not have any protection of our individual rights— life, liberty, and property. There would either be too much government oversight or the opposite extreme, none at all. The Constitution ensured solid boundaries and limits were established between the government and its people. In other words, without the Constitution, we would be living in total chaos.

The Constitution and all of its subsequent Amendments consist of a mere 4,500 words. When completed, the book you are holding in your hands is likely to be ten times that size! There is a lot packed into our Constitution. It is a paragon of concision, containing a Preamble, seven Articles, and twenty-seven Amendments. That's it: no rhetoric, no fluff, no wasted words.

The Preamble
We all know how the preamble begins (or at least we think we do):

> *We the People of the United States, in Order to form a more perfect Union, establish Justice, insure domestic Tranquility, provide for the common defense, promote*

the general Welfare, and secure the Blessings of Liberty to ourselves and our Posterity, do ordain and establish this Constitution for the United States of America.

Simple, elegant, and to the point. This document is for *us, all Americans* ("We the People"). We agree to honor lawfulness ("Justice"), peace ("domestic Tranquility"), protection ("the common defense"), freedom ("Blessings and Liberty"), and health ("general Welfare"). I don't see anything that could be misinterpreted in any way or a single mention of a political party, do you?

Note that in the above I bolded the first letter of words that have been capitalized in the actual Constitution. Evidently, they were the words our framers believed deserved extra attention as proper nouns. We can only speculate why the two words "common defense" were the only ones *not* capitalized. Perhaps, it was some form of subliminal message from our Founding Fathers that military strength was not nearly as important as the other principles? (The answer may be even more simple than that—a typo—though I doubt it. Franklin was a printer on top of all of his other endeavors and a pretty meticulous fellow; I doubt he'd allow an oversight like that to slip through.)

The Seven Articles

Next comes what has become known as The Seven Articles. These outline the branches of government and provide insight into how our framers believed the parts should operate. These are The Seven Articles at a glance:

Article I: The Legislative Branch
- Specifies who creates the laws: Congress
- Divides Congress into the Senate and the House of Representatives

- Establishes the rules on how members should be elected

Article II: The Executive Branch
- Outlines the responsibilities of the President and Vice President and how these individuals are expected to roll out the laws
- Lays out how the election process should work
- Sets the boundaries of Presidential power
- Provides a framework for the impeachment process, if deemed necessary

Article III: The Judicial Branch
- Establishes the Supreme Court
- Itemizes the duties and powers of the Supreme Court, as well as the federal courts
- Addresses the power of judicial review
- Defines what constitutes treasonous acts against the country

Article IV: The States
- Provides the rules on how states are admitted to the Union
- Details how states are designed get along with other states
- Offers guarantees to states

Article V: Making Amendments
- Explains how Amendments may be added to the Constitution

Article VI: Supreme Law of the Land
- Reasserts that United States Constitution is the highest law of the land

Article VII: Ratification
- States the approval of the entire document

Let's boil the Articles down to what the framers had in mind by establishing equal parts of our government: defining areas of purview and how the entities should work together; specifying how laws are created, approved, and executed; and providing checks and balances to ensure one area of government doesn't overreach its authority or break the law.

The Articles don't address the needs or wants of any political party—and with good reason. Our Founding Fathers clearly did not want a government in which one party had *carte blanche* domination and rule over the other.

The message is clear: The *people* rule and the officials are civil servants.

I liken the Articles to an "instruction manual" that comes with a board game, such as Monopoly. It's up to the players themselves to read the instructions and then understand, interpret, and enforce them. If you fail to obey the rules, you go to jail, do not pass go, or collect $200. (Okay, I admit that part is specific to Monopoly.)

The Twenty-Seven Amendments
These are The Twenty-Seven Constitutional Amendments:

I	Freedom of religion, speech, press, assembly, petition
II	Right to bear arms
III	Quartering of troops
IV	Search and seizure
V	Due process, double jeopardy, self-incrimination
VI	Jury trial, right to counsel
VII	Common lawsuits

VIII	Excess bail or fines; cruel and unusual punishment
IX	Rights not named
X	Powers reserved to states
XI	Lawsuits against a state
XII	Election of President and Vice President
XIII	Abolition of slavery
XIV	Due process, equal protection, privileges of citizens
XV	Rights not to be denied because of race
XVI	Income tax
XVII	Election of senators
XVIII	Prohibition
XIX	Women's right to vote
XX	Presidential term and succession
XXI	Repeal of Prohibition
XXII	President limited to two terms
XXIII	Right to vote for President and Vice President and for persons in D.C.
XXIV	No poll tax
XXV	Presidential succession
XXVI	Right to vote at age eighteen
XXVII	Compensation for members of Congress

Once again, there is no mention of political party in any way, shape, or form. More remarkably, of the twenty-seven Amendments, only one was downright foolish (#18, Prohibition), and later on it ended up being repealed (#21). (Some might also argue that #27, compensation for members of Congress, should also be repealed, but that would be in jest.) And there is only one (#2, the Right to Bear Arms) that is a continuous source of debate in the present day, mainly because times have changed over the last couple of centuries and gun violence involving Americans shooting other Americans has risen.

Often Americans look at the squabbling, mudslinging, and stalemates taking place on a daily basis in Washington, D.C. without taking into account how well our Constitution has been serving us throughout all of these years. Is it perfect? No. Does it have all of the answers? Of course not. How could minds even as brilliant as Madison, Washington, Hamilton, and Franklin have been expected to anticipate such things as our nation's massive expansion, population growth, technological advancements, globalism, and environmental crises? They certainly could not have envisioned a country that would ultimately be divided by Red States vs. Blue States. To be sure, however, they had astonishing foresight and, for the most part, hit the mark with the document. We generally falter when we ignore or misinterpret the Constitution for political advantage and rely on uncivility rather than coming together to discuss our differences in the tradition of our Founding Fathers.

WHY THE STARS AND STRIPES, THE PLEDGE OF ALLEGIANCE, AND "THE STAR-SPANGLED BANNER" STILL MATTER

American principles are questioned and challenged every day—and they should be. As we've established, we are a free country and have the right to express our opinions and views. There are also limits to personal freedoms, as expressed in the writings of figures such as British philosopher John Stuart Mill and American Associate Supreme Court Justice Oliver Wendell Holmes. In 1882, John B. Finch, Chairman of the Prohibition National Committee, reportedly said, "…your right to swing your arm leaves off where my right not to have my nose struck begins."

This above is meant figuratively and literally. Essentially, you have the freedom to blindfold yourself and wave a large stick in any direction until you whack someone on the nose or damage his or her property. If you are guilty of these actions, you have broken the law and must pay the consequences.

That seems pretty easy to understand and interpret. But—and here comes the gray area—where do things such as respect for our country and sensitivity to our nation's patriots come in? Is flag burning okay to protest an unjust war? Can a grade school student refuse to say the Pledge of Allegiance because "under God" conflicts with her religious beliefs? And—here's the biggest can of worms I'm opening—is it justifiable for an athlete to take a knee during the singing of our national anthem to protest racial injustice? (Attention: NFL player Colin Kaepernick in 2016).

The stars and stripes of our flag matter.
Our Pledge of Allegiance matters.
"The Star-Spangled Banner" matters.

All of the above are important symbols of our national pride, strength, and unity. I was a soldier myself, having served in Vietnam and I am proud of all of our symbols and patriotic statements and songs. I completely relate to and understand why veterans, soldiers, and government officials would be personally offended by blatant disrespect to our flag and our national anthem—both of which I honor and love with all of my heart.

But, going back to John Finch's quote, did Colin Kaepernick strike someone's nose? Did his action of taking a knee warrant his being ostracized by the NFL and merit nasty Tweets by our President? I disagree wholeheartedly with how the athlete expressed his opinion and do feel it was disrespectful and unnecessary. I, for one, would have much preferred he had written an Op Ed column in *The New York Times* rather than making such a public display. But who am I to judge his action? I am not in his shoes and can't fairly balance his outcry for equality vs. the patriotic need for respect. Therefore, I don't believe the attacks against him were warranted. It turned into a political play and everyone seemed to take sides, which is why the whole thing blew completely out of proportion.

Respect must go both ways. We need *to listen* to each other. We must honor the wisdom of our Founding Fathers and Mothers. This means turning the American ship around and re-learning how to conduct political discourse and, on occasion, disagreeing with civility.

With this in mind, we are now ready to address the Ten Principles: *Vision. Leadership. Truth-Seeking. Courage. Integrity. Tolerance and Equality. Respect. Patriotism. Capitalism and Money. Compromise.*

Let's get to work.

PART TWO

The Ten Principles

The Foundation of every government
is some principle or passion
in the minds of the people.

—*John Adams, 2nd President of the United States*

PRINCIPLE #1: *Vision*

Ask not what your country can do for you;
ask what you can do for your country.

—*John F. Kennedy, 35th President of the United States*

I can't over-emphasize the urgency of our nation and its leaders to create and sustain a unified *Vision*. It is so crucial that, by intent, I have strategically placed it as the first Principle.

Our Founding Fathers and Mothers had a unique vision for America as they built its foundations from the ground up. It may be summarized in three simple words:

We the People.

There is no possible way to misinterpret the above three words. The incisive message says it all: The government works *for* the people—*all* of the people and never the other way around. By government, we mean the Presidential, Legislative, and Judicial branches. Politicians invariably forget the fact that they were elected by us, the people, and that they report to us and are paid by us. It's abundantly clear that no one—not even the President—is ever above the law.

Our colonial leaders cherished the concept of governance for and by the people and understood the necessity of establishing a balance of power, known as checks and balances, among the three respective branches. The one thing that seemed to make President George Washington's flesh crawl was the idea of being dubbed a "king." He didn't wish to wield any more power than was necessary to conduct his business as President. He viewed himself as something of a servant of the people.

President Washington not only honored the *We the People Vision* of America, he believed in it with all of his heart and soul. Everything he accomplished as President fed into this vision. Without his leadership and example, the original *Vision* might possibly have been diluted, manipulated, or outright disobeyed, in which case all of the masterful work done by the Founding Fathers would have gone to waste and the country would not be what it is today.

Everything stems from a vision, whether we are referring to our personal lives, our businesses, or even our government. I don't care who you are or what you do: It is essential for there to always be a powerful vision supported from the top (even if it's you in your personal life), or else the "dream" (i.e., the desired end result) will become mere fantasy and fail to come to fruition.

VISION QUEST

In business—whether it's a corporation, a privately-owned business, a small business, or even a nonprofit—*Vision* is often confused with *Purpose*, *Mission*, *Values*, and *Strategy*. While they all must work together in harmony and sometimes overlap, each of these statements serves a different and equally as valuable a role to ensure everyone is rowing in the same direction. When one person rows counter to everyone else, the boat tips, rocks, and goes off-course. Someone may even fall (or get pushed) overboard. Our government is no different in terms of the ideology behind how the boat must be rowed.

Let's simplify things by looking at these distinctions:

- *Vision:* where the entity is going in the future; where we would like it to be at the end of the journey.

- *Purpose:* why the journey is meaningful; what drives us to move forward with passion.

- *Mission:* what must be accomplished during the journey; how this distinguishes our entity from others.

- *Values:* what are the common concerns the majority shares with heart and soul; what we stand for and represent.

- *Strategy:* how the *Vision, Purpose,* and *Mission* will be accomplished while maintaining our core *Values*; the actions we take to fulfill our desired goals.

Due to the scope of this book, we are only going to focus on *Vision*. That doesn't make the other areas any less important, and I promise I will give all of them their due in a later work down the road.

The greatest minds and creative talents in all areas of human endeavor had unparalleled visions: Abraham Lincoln, Albert Einstein, Winston Churchill, John F. Kennedy, The Beatles, Steve Jobs, and many others. There were several factors that made all of their visions (which we'll get to, don't worry) stand out:

1. Universal appeal on both the individual and group level

2. Implication that it presents the best possible future

3. Statement of a bold promise

4. Evidence that it provides a powerful service to the individual and to the larger group

5. Simplicity of message

6. Clarity of message

7. Constant communication of the message

8. Consistency of message

9. Authenticity among those who preach it

10. Obsession with making the *Vision* come true

Now let's take a closer look at the unique visions of all the aforementioned leaders:

Abraham Lincoln: *A house divided against itself cannot stand.*
- Message: Preserve the Union at all costs.

Albert Einstein: *Imagination is more important than knowledge.*
- Message: Science doesn't have any limitations or boundaries.

Winston Churchill: *We shall go on to the end, we shall fight in France, we shall fight on the seas and oceans, we shall fight with growing confidence and growing strength in the air, we shall defend our Island, whatever the cost may be, we shall fight on*

the beaches, we shall fight on the landing grounds,
we shall fight in the fields and in the streets, we shall
fight in the hills; we shall never surrender....

- Message: We are going to defy the odds and win this war, no matter what.

John F. Kennedy: *Ask not what your country can do for you; ask what you can do for your country.*
- Message: Contribute to the public good.

The Beatles: *All you need is love.*
- Message: Our generation is united through peace and love.

Steve Jobs: *Think different.*
- Message: Apple's products change lives.

The ten factors I referenced earlier hold true in all of these vision statements. The examples are concise, simple, direct, effective, and universal and yet, in precious few words, pack powerful emotions that are easy to communicate and comprehend. There is no mistaking the meaning of "All You Need Is Love" when you hear it played (or the lyrics to John Lennon's "Imagine" as well). When a vision is crafted right, it is a work of art that everyone admires, treasures, accepts, and follows. The people who embrace the vision have come to accept it as theirs because they are confident in the leader's authenticity; they mean what they say.

A certain pride is also associated with believing wholeheartedly in the vision, which is why it is so vital in the world of politics. Leaders must attract and win over an enormous number of supporters, voters, and constituents in order to be elected and maintain the base; this may only be accomplished with a strong unifying vision.

Once the vision has been fully established, it becomes a symbol of what the leader, the administration, and often the business entity stand for to the employees within the organization and to the broader public and stakeholders. Many companies will prominently display a vision statement on the wall right when you enter the lobby or reception, as well as on the company website. In this fashion, no one can ever claim he or she doesn't know the company's vision—i.e., where the company is headed in the future. This repeated emphasis helps the political administration or employees of a business (whichever the case may be) from the top on down endure challenges and serve as a reminder of what is important, especially when it comes to decision-making and answering the question: "Does it fit in with our vision?" If it doesn't, maybe the answer should be *No*. An organization should only engage in creative action that serves to establish or reinforce the vision, even if it's a good idea.

Eventually, the vision becomes second nature by people throughout the organization "walking the walk and talking the talk." This all goes back to repetition and consistency; if the leaders reiterate the message at every turn, it becomes part of the fabric of the culture. The wonderful upside is that, when the leaders need the masses to rally together most, the people are right behind him or her because they are already emotionally connected to the vision. The most enduring vision statements can weather any storm and guide teams—and an entire nation, for that matter—to overcoming any challenge.

And there's more—a lot more, especially when it comes to how our elected officials approach and unveil their visions in this day and age. One would think that each and every one of them—especially in the highest office of President—would honor the legacy of our Founding Fathers' *We the People*, as well the legacy of those who followed them. Unfortunately, as we know all too well, that has not always been the case.

VISION: MORE THAN MEETS THE EYE

In politics, campaign slogans often get straight to the heart of the candidate's vision. President Barack Obama had several messages: "Yes, We Can," "Change We Can Believe In," and "Hope." Prior to his presidency, President George W. Bush had a couple of slogans in his two sequential campaigns: "Compassionate Conservativism" and "A Safer World and a More Hopeful America." All of these slogans were highly effective for both men because they fit the ten criteria stated earlier in the chapter, link (at least in some tangible way) to *We the People,* and reflect the authentic ideology of each politician.

Now let's see some examples of political visions gone awry.

Is "America First" a Shared Vision?

One of the slogans of 2004 Democratic Party presidential candidate John Kerry was "A Stronger America." A good slogan? Absolutely. But did the message resonate as a strong vision? I would say *not* because more Americans identified the Republican candidate (President George W. Bush) as the person who was equipped to "make America stronger." Kerry's slogan lacked authenticity. His alternate slogan, "Let America Be America Again," seems pretty abstract and flat, which is no doubt why it was ineffective. Ultimately, he lost the election (though not just for these reasons).

Let's flash forward to the controversial 2016 presidential election (although one might say that *all* elections are controversial). Whether you support President Donald J. Trump or not, there is no denying that his two main campaign slogans—"America First" and "Make America Great Again"—were successful in terms of building his base and garnering votes.

But…were they really unique visions for America? I would suggest *not* for several reasons. Let's begin with the obvious first issue, originality: Neither President Donald J. Trump nor his campaigners created either slogan.

Yes, you've read that right. Both slogans were borrowed from earlier political campaigns. "America First" was actually coined by Republican candidate Pat Buchanan in 1992. "Let's Make America Great Again" was used by Republican President Ronald Reagan in 1984.

Coincidence? Probably not—but we don't need to explore that further. If originality is not a problem for you, then let's focus on the other issues with the slogans as representative visions for our country—none of which has anything to do with political party or policy. Mark my words, however: The failure of these two slogans to serve as visions for America are partially behind why our country has become so fractured.

A major shortcoming of "America First"—for both Pat Buchanan and, more recently, President Trump—is that it breaks with a cardinal rule: *Our allies matter.* Any vision must also include our allies, much like sales accounts, vendors, and customers should be welcomed into the extended family in a business. The better these relationships are served, the stronger our nation becomes when we need them (or vice versa). When we are involved in any conflict—whether it's with North Korea, Russia, or any Middle Eastern country—we rely upon our allies in terms of political support, negotiations, military aid, intelligence, and many other things.

"America First" essentially tells other nations: "You're on your own, buddy." While it is perfectly fine to say, "We need to leverage improved trade agreements with our allies," it is *not* all right to upset our valued relationships with them—many of whom fought alongside our troops in World War I, World War II, the Korean War, the Vietnam War, and other conflicts. Meanwhile, "America First" has now also evolved to signify President Trump's pullouts from the treaty with Iran (a broken promise) and the Paris Agreement to save our planet.

According to the Global Carbon Project, the United States is the global leader in one thing: CO_2 emission. (China, by the way—which has a much larger population—is third on the list.) As a country, America produces 5.1 billion metric tons of energy-related carbon dioxide out of the world's total of 32.5 billion metric tons. So, we produce one-sixth of the world's CO_2 but won't do anything to help battle climate change? In other words, we make the mess and then won't help clean it up. America used to be a world leader on issues such as this; we could inspire others to follow our example. Apparently, this is no longer the case.

"America First" is also contrarian to America's role as a leader of the free world, a nation that is welcoming to people who wish to enter from other countries. America is, in fact, a nation of immigrants—and Native Americans are the only true original people of this great land (which is a controversy for another day). Our Founding Fathers prized the idea of America being a haven for people who faced religious persecution in their own countries and one that allows citizens to practice whatever religion they wish.

While I agree that we must strengthen and protect our borders against threats such as terrorism and drug cartels, I do not believe the way to do is to insult Mexico, our ally, by building an unnecessary wall between the two countries. President Trump's slurs about Mexicans (i.e., "bad *hombres*" and "rapists") and attempts to ban people who have certain religious beliefs is the exact opposite of what our nation stands for. As is stated on our Lady Liberty:

Give me your tired, your poor, Your huddled masses yearning to breathe free, The wretched refuse of your teeming shore, Send these, the homeless, tempest-tost to me, I lift my lamp beside the golden door!

America's Greatness Resides within Its People

The second logo from President Trump, "Make America Great Again," is problematic on a number of fronts. Mainly, America's status was vastly different when President Reagan took office in 1980 vs. when President Donald Trump did the same in 2016. When President Ronald Reagan said, "Let's Make America Great Again," our country had been suffering through high inflation and low economic growth. The country felt the sting of the energy crisis and low consumer confidence. The Iran hostage crisis made America feel weak and helpless against our foes.

Then President Reagan came on the scene: strong, confident, witty, and with all-new ideas about governing that vastly differed from his predecessor, President Jimmy Carter. The country rallied behind President Reagan's vision and, whether imagined or not, we once again felt powerful—a country that was not to be messed with.

Flash forward to 2016 when President Trump took office. The prior leader of our country, President Obama, set the policy that guided us out of a major Recession. Without his leadership, America would have fallen into an all-out Depression. Generally speaking, employment and the stock market rebounded. Although his administration was imperfect, President Obama nationalized health care for millions of people who didn't have medical insurance coverage and helped push forward the Paris Accord.

Where, exactly, was the perception that America was *not* great? Certainly, there were things that needed improvement—the national debt and the GDP, to name a couple—but, on the whole, things were better for the country after President Obama left office than before.

In addition to the circumstances being different in the Reagan vs. Trump eras, the slogans themselves also varied. How so? President Reagan proclaimed, "Let's Make America Great Again," whereas President Trump snipped off the all-important first word: *Let's*.

On the surface, the distinction seems minor—but it is not. Remember, the vision of our Founding Fathers was *We the People*. President Reagan's slogan was all-inclusive for every single American: *Let's Make America Great Again*. In other words, we are invited to be in this effort together: Republicans, Democrats, and everyone else.

By stating *Make America Great Again*—and symbolizing it with the cultish red hat—President Trump was only speaking to his base, which was perhaps 40% of the American population. What about the other 60%? Essentially, he was spouting that only ardent Trump voters were part of his vision to make America great again. Everyone else could go to…well, you can only guess where he had in mind.

The other ill-conceived part of this vision is that *Make America Great Again* sounds distinctly like a direct order barked from Mount Olympus up above. By use of the action verb "make" to begin the slogan, President Trump was commanding people to do his bidding. Whatever happened to the sacred idea that *the government works for the people*? President Trump clearly believes it's the other way around and that we work for him. As of this writing during President Trump's first term, he has not made one single attempt to listen to people outside his party and govern for the entire country. He keeps people in line by bullying and threatening them through his Twitter feed: He leads through *fear*. The fact that President Trump continues to don the hat at his rallies is further evidence of how he excludes non-supporters by riling up his cult-like following. President George Washington is no doubt rolling in his grave at the idea of a President in office playing the role of king and issuing intimidating commands from a throne with a red cap as a crown.

Principle #1, *Vision*, is the starting point for what America must do to right the ship. We need a vision that is true and speaks to *every citizen*, not just the people who voted for the candidate. Once a leader takes an oath of office, he or she must then create a universal vision that has meaning and resonates for all Americans.

The right vision must also speak to excellence—how we can work together to create a bright future for everyone, not just the wealthy or any other group. This vision must include positive words that *unite* the country, not split the red and blue seams even wider apart.

I believe that the right vision for America is something special, something wonderful, and something we can all embrace and agree upon. It may come from a Republican, a Democrat, or an Independent. It may be created and communicated by a person who is not of the same gender, race, religion, or sexual orientation as you, the reader. I, for one, do not care about any of this—as long as it furthers the message of *We the People* and celebrates our huddled masses.

Now that we see things clearly with a proper understanding of *Vision*, we are able to move on to the second principle, *Leadership*. Before you turn the page, be mindful of this important point: Leadership is not a welcome invitation to accumulate power. Friends, the following is not in any way a radical socialist sentiment, but rather, an idea that goes back to our Founding Fathers: *power to the people!*

PRINCIPLE #2: *Leadership*

A great statesman is he who knows
when to depart from traditions,
as well as when to adhere to them.

—*John Stuart Mill, British philosopher*

O ver the years, I have served as a transformational coach to numerous leaders in a variety of industries. Through my Circle of Success® (COS) program, these leaders have learned: how to inspire, empower, encourage, and challenge others; what attributes are essential for development and growth; what responsibilities they must assume; what are their strengths and weakness (derived from 360-degree feedback); and more.

I don't believe the world of politics is all that different from business in terms of determining what it takes to be a great leader. Unfortunately, however, zero to precious few politicians elected to office ever consider professional leadership coaching and training. Why do you suppose that is? I would venture to explain in the following manner: 1) no one ever obligates them to do it; 2) the training isn't as accessible to them; 3) they don't make the time for it; or 4) they don't feel they need it and therefore don't bother.

Regarding #4: It goes without saying that people who run for office usually have plenty of ego to spare. To some extent, a certain amount of hubris and a thick skin are requisites for those assuming a government position in order to withstand constant public scrutiny. Their entire private, professional, and personal lives inevitably end up exposed, and pretty much everyone on the planet has some skeleton he or she wishes to keep locked away in the far reaches of a dark closet.

These are the foremost questions on my mind: *Do today's political leaders have what it takes to drive our nation? Do they even have a smidgeon of the knowledge, skill, and talent of our Founding Fathers to continue the legacy?* Tragically, the answers are plain as day: *no* and *no*.

In Principle #2, *Leadership*, we will first review the dozen criteria all political leaders must have to some degree in order to help guide our nation back on its proper course. You'll note some of these are so important they stand out on their own as individual principles we will cover later on in this book.

THE DIVINE DOZEN: POLITICAL LEADERSHIP CRITERIA

In many contemporary cases, we've seen leaders who demonstrate a few of my Political Leadership Criteria; however, they don't exemplify them well enough to compensate for those they don't have. To be sure, I can't think of any modern politicians who rise to a level anywhere near our Founding Fathers when it comes to these attributes.

Without further ado, here they are:

1. Has a clear, unifying vision

2. Recognizes potential in others

3. Develops trust

4. Encourages excellence

5. Exhibits integrity

6. Shows empathy

7. Maintains a sense of humor

8. Demonstrates humility

9. Conveys passion

10. Exudes confidence

11. Displays courage

12. Radiates style

Now let's examine them one at a time with an eye toward Presidents who serve as prime examples and those who do not.

Has a Clear, Unifying Vision

As explained in Principle #1, political candidates usually have a vision in tandem with their campaigns that appeal to their bases and convince others to hop on the bandwagon. Once in office, however, the vision needs to be amended to include *all* Americans—not just any one party or sector. Think of it this way: Everyone pays taxes, which end up in the paychecks of our government officials. Whether we voted for a candidate or not, we still pay the same taxes that line the pockets of these elected officials. Now, I don't think I'm being naïve here. I fully recognize that politicians have campaign promises to fulfill, donors to placate, and constituents to please. However, the overarching vision of every politician must be inclusive of people from all areas within the individual's purview. Once the vision has been established, the elected official must repeatedly convey it to countrymen and women in a way that is clear, concise, and consistent. Individuals in this community should understand *why* this vision is so important, *what* it means to the average citizen, and *how* it will be rolled out.

The following are some global leaders throughout history who had brilliant visions for their nations: Greek King Alexander the Great, Roman Emperor Julius Caesar, Egyptian Queen Cleopatra, UK Queen Elizabeth I, Russian Empress Catherine the Great, President George Washington, President Abraham Lincoln, President Theodore Roosevelt, President Franklin Delano Roosevelt, President John F. Kennedy, Israeli Prime Minister Golda Meir, UK Prime Minister Winston Churchill, President Ronald Reagan, and South African President Nelson Mandela.

There are also several figures who did not hold an official office but would most certainly qualify due to their contributions to their respective social realms, including: Jesus Christ, Martin Luther King Jr., Mother Teresa, Mohandas Gandhi, Pope Francis, and the Dalai Lama.

What's missing? Leaders who have a grand, unified future for America in the here and now. We are far too fractured and segmented with political visions that only appeal to 50% of the country at most. We need a leader who can create a vision that binds us back together again. For starters, how about this: *Let's Make America UNITED Again*. I like it so much I may trademark it for myself!

Recognizes Potential in Others

In business, it's crucial for leaders to hire the best possible candidates, assign the right people to the right roles, and foster talent. When it comes to political posts, the idea is similar but not exact. A politician (usually) doesn't go through a Human Resources department or Indeed.com to recruit people for his or her staff, and the vetting process is different. There may be background checks and such—especially for positions that require security clearances—but, on the whole, politicians have the luxury of hiring whomever they choose, including friends, family, donors, and political cronies.

Such freedom has its pros and cons. Since political leaders often don't have to go through so many hoops in the recruiting process, they hire people they know and trust; those they believe share their common principles and values; wealthy people who donate to their campaigns; and others who simply impress them on the spot. More than ever, there is a great deal of nepotism involved: politicians who hire insiders and even family members to important posts without their having the requisite knowledge and experience. For these reasons and due to a general lack of overall scrutiny, we've consistently seen political assignees become embroiled in a litany of scandals at every level and branch of government.

On the opposite end of the spectrum, I believe leaders—politicians included—are responsible for not only hiring exceptional talent to fill their staff positions from top to bottom, they should be equally charged with identifying the stars and empowering them with increasing amounts of responsibility. This could be anyone from an intern all of the way up to a chief of staff. The leader is only as good as the team and will only achieve great things when the women and men advising him or her are recognized and provided with encouragement.

In the world of politics, it's often difficult to separate recognition that is awarded to loyalists versus those who have accomplished exceptional things. There are "Yes" men and women in every type of professional environment, and political leaders must be wary of this. Are the brownnosers saying what their bosses want to hear, or are they giving it to them straight? In the former situation, they aren't doing any favors to their superiors.

Most Presidents, except for Donald J. Trump, have hired cabinet members with substantial government experience. The cabinets of G.H.W. Bush, Bill Clinton, G.W. Bush, and Barack Obama were in the 81-91% prior experience range, whereas to date Trump has hired only 57% with previous government roles. True enough, he pledged to "drain the swamp" and bring a business sensibility to Washington, D.C. which he accomplished in terms of posting non-Washington insiders. For better or worse, nearly one quarter of his appointments were CEOs (significantly higher than all four of his predecessors).

On the opposite end of the spectrum, Obama and Clinton appointed PhDs to nearly a quarter of their positions, alongside the high percentage of individuals with previous government experience. I, for one, strongly believe that education and experience are pretty strong indicators of good hires—even if you wish to "drain the swamp." If you were President, wouldn't you want to be surrounded by smart people who knew a thing a two about how to handle the roles they were undertaking? Our Founding Fathers— Washington, Adams, Jefferson, Franklin, Madison, Hamilton, et al—were indisputably *brilliant* men for their time (albeit not PhDs). Trump described Rex Tillerson, his appointed Secretary of State, as being "dumb as a rock." If this were true, shouldn't Trump have been aware of this when he initially hired him?

Either way, mocking a former cabinet member (or anyone, for that matter) is disrespectful and unbecoming of a true leader. Certainly, it doesn't speak well of his ability to recognize and nurture talent. Trump's staggeringly high turnover rate in appointees—82% in his first three and a half years—far exceeds any other President in recent history. According to a 2016 Compensation Force Study, the average turnover rate in business is just under 18%. If President Trump has been running our country like a business, it's the most chaotic enterprise we have ever witnessed.

There is no surefire way to rate how well political leaders recognize potential. A lot happens behind the scenes that we don't see or hear about. One measure, perhaps, is which direct reports accomplish remarkable things and successfully advance to the next office. For example, John F. Kennedy's Vice President, Lyndon B. Johnson, became President after the former was assassinated. Although Johnson's Presidency was controversial during his time due to civil unrest and America's involvement in the Vietnam War, he accomplished many remarkable things during his tenure, including: signing off on a tax cut; pushing through the Clean Air and Civil Rights Acts; and establishing Medicare and Medicaid.

There are other notable examples. President Reagan was succeeded by his Vice President, G.H. Bush, who served a successful term of office. Although Bill Clinton's Vice President, Al Gore, narrowly lost his Presidential election bid (to G.W. Bush), he went on to win a Nobel Prize for his efforts with the Intergovernmental Panel on Climate Change.

Truly great leaders are never intimidated or threatened by bringing in smart people who can get the job done.

Develops Trust

As it happens, Principle #3 focuses directly on truth-telling, so we won't get into elaborate detail on the subject, except with regard to leadership.

When it comes to the world of business, corporate boards, shareholders, employees, customers, and vendors all look to a company's leadership for trustworthiness. The subject has become even more imperative in recent years; so much so, in fact, that Stephen M.R. Covey devoted a whole book to it: *The Speed of Trust: The One Thing That Changes Everything*. If trust in leadership doesn't exist within an organization, the staff looks for jobs elsewhere; morale sinks; in-fighting occurs among the ranks; sales plummet; and partners don't want to engage with the company.

Trust can be eroded in a heartbeat with just one scandal—whether it's financial-related or in the realm of moral turpitude. With the #MeToo Movement and criminal cases involving several prominent people who have fallen from grace (Harvey Weinstein, Matt Lauer, Bill O'Reilly, and Roger Ailes, to name a few), companies and HR departments are on close guard for anything smacking of impropriety, malfeasance, and inappropriateness. When in doubt, companies dismiss these executives (sometimes having to pay them off with a golden parachute in order to hasten their exits).

What about trust when it comes to politics? Ha! I know you are laughing at the words "trust" and "politics" being in the same sentence, as they seem contradictory. I mentioned in the Preface that some people think politicians are "paid to lie." Well, even politicians themselves have been known to be glib about the subject:

I trust no one, not even myself.

—JOSEPH STALIN, Premier of the Soviet Union

Trust but verify.

—PRESIDENT RONALD REAGAN

It's good to trust others but, not to do so is much better.

—BENITO MUSSOLINI, Prime Minister of Italy

All kidding aside, how should political leaders stack up on the subject of trust? While I believe there needs to be a pretty high level of trust between government leaders and the people, I am also realistic about the fact that sometimes it is in the best interests of protecting national security to fudge things a bit, if the situation calls for it. However, when it comes to "protecting your butt"—such as from a scandal—I take the opposite stance. Leaders must have a level of transparency on these matters, even sensitive ones, or else public trust in government gets lost.

Let's think about it this way: The President has access to the nuclear football containing the access codes that could destroy an entire nation. If we don't trust the President, his or her access to those codes can be a pretty frightening scenario to picture. The same holds true for handling international peace talks, decisions regarding taxation and the economy, individual liberties, and much more.

Trust can be a personal and touchy subject—and subjective, too. For example, at least half of Americans today would claim that President Donald Trump is the least trustworthy President in our history, whereas his base of supporters would argue the exact opposite. I assert, however, we can all agree that President Bill Clinton would score fairly low on the trust-meter across the board (having been impeached for lying under oath), as would President Richard Nixon (who stepped down before facing the impeachment vote and earned the nickname "Tricky Dickie").

Now for the all-important question: Which modern-day President might rate highly in terms of trust? Ironically, President Jimmy Carter would score quite well in terms of trust; however, he was honest to such a fault (if such a thing is possible) that it actually weakened America in several respects.

Presidents also serve as military leaders and, for this reason, they sometimes must be "sly as foxes" in order to achieve a desired result during troubling times. Indeed,

President "Honest Abe" Lincoln was such a figure. Having been a shrewd attorney, Lincoln was also a cunning leader and superb manipulator of the law. During extraordinary circumstances, such as the Civil War and the fight to abolish slavery, he recognized that desperate means were necessary. Lincoln was one of the few figures who could successfully tow that line—but he paid a steep price for his principles by receiving a bullet to his head one fateful night at Ford's Theatre in Washington, D.C.

Encourages Excellence

America prides itself on its breadth of accomplishments in countless areas. We look to achieve excellence when it comes to technology, innovation, space flight, business growth, military strength, and more.

Yet how do our government leaders fare in terms of encouraging strong performance from others? Not too well, I'm afraid. In many cases, it's every woman and man out for him or herself. The following nasty, albeit hilarious quote from VP Selina Meyer (portrayed by Julia Louis-Dreyfus) in the satirical TV show *Veep* in reference to character Jonah Ryan (Timothy Ryan), a White House liaison, says it all: "You let that unstable piece of human scaffolding into your house?"

We can examine the ability to encourage excellence in at least a couple of ways. As with the previous section on recognizing potential in others, we might look at the notable successes within the political administrations. For all of his faults, President Nixon made a wise decision choosing Henry Kissinger as his Secretary of State, rewarding him with a lot of space in which to perform his duties establishing the country's foreign policy. Nixon was even known to give Kissinger a boost of praise every now and then: "[He is] a man who has the poise and strength and character to serve in this great position."

Under Obama's administration, the President and his Vice President, Joe Biden, had a famous public bromance. They were often photographed laughing together and hugging and seemed to have been unified on almost every issue. On presenting Biden with the Medal of Freedom, Obama lavished the following praise upon him: "We all know that on its own, his work does not capture the full measure of Joe Biden.... When Joe talks about opportunity for our children, we hear the father who rode the rails home every night so he could be there to tuck his kids into bed.... When Joe talks to Gold Star families who've lost a hero, we hear another father of an American veteran.... A resilient, and loyal, and humble servant...."

By the same token, up until the COVID-19 crisis, President Trump was stone-cold silent about his Vice President, Mike Pence. It's impossible to get inside the mind of the President, but to the public, it appears one of several things might be happening: he didn't want his VP to be empowered and receive any credit he expects for himself; he didn't trust his VP; or, he was waiting to see if he needs to throw his VP under the bus for something (such as leading the COVID-19 team).

In the meantime, VP Pence does what everyone in this President's circle feels he or she must do in order to convince the President of his loyalty: lavish praise upon his boss. In one cabinet meeting, Pence gushed about his President no less than every twelve and a half seconds. This one is a doozy: "Because of your leadership, Mr. President, and because of the strong support of the leadership in the Congress of the United States, you're delivering on that middle-class miracle."

Suffice it to say, I believe that great leaders should complement their staffs—not the other way around. A true leader should not have any need for sycophants buzzing around all of the time like drones around a queen bee.

Another route to evaluating excellence is how a leader inspires excellence within the country as an entity. If the temperature of the nation feels *blah,* as was the case under the Herbert Hoover (who held office during the Great Depression) and Jimmy Carter administrations, we know something is off-track.

Let's return to President Reagan as a fine example of how to lead by pumping up the nation's strengths and abilities. Citizens as a whole felt Reagan had our backs and wanted all of us to succeed. In the mid-1980's, when America was faced with a serious economic threat from a flood of Japanese imported electronics and vehicles, Reagan took specific measures to counter it. He imposed tariffs on Japan's electronic products to level out the playing field and "enforce the principles of free and fair trade."

That was not all. In December 1985, Reagan established "Made in America Month" to increase the purchase of products created by American companies on our soil. Not only did this change consumer mindset and help American companies (and, by extension, the economy), it inspired citizens to take pride in our work as a country. Labels were sewn into clothes that were Made in America. Print, radio, and television advertising touted products that were Made in America. In the American conversation, people talked about how they would only "buy American" automobiles. To summarize: The message was received, accepted, and spread: *Americans strive to achieve excellence.*

Reagan's specific words lifted American spirits and helped us regain our confidence and swagger. Unlike many politicians on both sides of the aisle today who would rather spew insults at various groups, Reagan praised *all Americans*—including immigrants, the working-class, farmers, and corporate America. Reagan's words continue to resonate today:

But America's producers are responding to that challenge, and it is time for consumers both here and abroad to take a fresh look at what America has to offer. Those who do will find the traditional variety, high quality, and dependability that "Made in the U.S.A." has come to symbolize.... In an increasingly competitive world, we Americans must redouble our efforts to make products of the highest quality in the most efficient way and market them aggressively. As we do, I have no doubt that more and more Americans and foreigners will be drawn to the products with the proud label: "Made in America."

Only one word can describe the above: *excellent.*

Exhibits Integrity

If you happen to have read through the Table of Contents and/or skipped on ahead to later principles, you are already aware that Integrity is Principle #5 and we will be touching upon that subject in totality before you know it.

Like Trust and Truth-telling, Integrity is also considered to be at odds when mentioned in the same breath as political leadership. Integrity does, in fact, overlap with honesty, but I believe there are important distinctions. I interpret integrity as standing for moral uprightness at all times. It means "walking the walk and talking the talk." Business professionals who get away with shady deals and then run victory laps afterward lose in the long run because people don't respect a person who lacks integrity; at some point, they will refuse to work alongside them. Leaders who exhibit integrity on a daily basis earn respect from others over time and gain supporters. Not only that, employees will follow those leaders to the ends of the earth and then embrace those values for themselves.

As previously mentioned, it only takes one misstep to

damage one's reputation. Once the act is exposed, the individual must make convincing apologies and work hard to earn back the label of having integrity. Right or wrong, some deeds and labels do become irreparable and can stick with a politician forever. Remember 1988 Democratic Presidential candidate Gary Hart? His romantic affair ruined what looked like a promising political career.

When a leader holds public office, temptation is everywhere in the form of power, greed, and sex. In this day and age of YouTube, iPhones, and social media, a life and career can be devastated with one click, and politicians must be extra guarded and vigilant. (It would be simpler for everyone to have a clean nose all of the time, but we know *that* is unlikely!) People are drawn to power like moths around a light bulb; once a politician has achieved such stature, he or she must walk around with a net and bug spray to stave off temptations that can lead to scandal. As nineteenth century British historian Sir John Dalberg-Acton famously said, "Power tends to corrupt, and power corrupts absolutely"; usually, this is shortened to "power corrupts."

Presidents John F. Kennedy and Bill Clinton, among others, were charismatic, handsome men who attracted women like magnets. President Donald Trump, by virtue of his businesses, brand, and public celebrity, had access to many beautiful women who saw him as a ticket to wealth and/or fame. The infidelities of these men have been well-documented, and I am not here to judge people for their promiscuity. They will be held accountable by their spouses and, someday perhaps, by their Maker.

On the other hand, a salacious or crooked leader becomes an object of global media ridicule, which reflects poorly on the integrity of our nation. By extension, America is made into a laughingstock. Is this how we choose to be regarded as a nation? I think not.

Shows Empathy

The political stereotypes go something like this: Democrats are touchy, feely, and compassionate (maternal, if you will), whereas Republicans are tough, protective, and aggressive (paternal). Taken to extremes, Democrats are "bleeding hearts," whereas Republicans are "greedy, insensitive war-mongers." Whether we are referencing a male or female political or business leader, you are probably wondering: *Why does empathy even matter?*

I will tell you why: Leaders—especially political figures—must wear many hats, but the most important one is *serving the people.* (Remember America's vision: *We the People.*) The voters elect the people into office. Taxpayers pay their salaries.

Yes, the President is the Commander-in-Chief when it comes to protecting the country and ensuring the safety of Americans. Equally as important is being present and sympathetic when unforeseen tragedy strikes. In the wake of epidemics, earthquakes, tsunamis, hurricanes, wildfires, mass shootings, and other tragedies, leaders are looked upon to help provide immediate medical support, financial aid, rescue operations, police protection, food/clothing/shelter, and other necessities. There is one more all-important thing the people expect from leadership: emotional support and comfort to victims and their families.

When the 9/11 terrorist attacks happened in New York City and thousands of lives were lost and many more wounded, where was Mayor Rudy Guiliani? He stood right on Ground Zero among the firefighters and officers while inhaling toxic fumes in order to report on whatever he could and provide kind, inspiring words to the devastated New York City community (and, in turn, the nation that was watching). As the Mayor said, "The attacks of September 11 were intended to break our spirit, instead we have emerged stronger and more unified. We feel renewed devotion to the principles of political, economic and religious freedom, the rule of law, and respect for human life. We are more determined than ever to live our lives in freedom."

Whatever we may think of Mayor Guiliani's more recent behavior, image, and politics, back in September 2001 he provided what was needed for that fragile time and place in history. He rallied New Yorkers together and helped them heal. He exemplified the leadership trait *empathy*.

By stark contrast, in November 2018, when the wildfires incinerated a significant portion of the Paradise, California forests, President Trump appeared on site and preached about how "raking and cleaning" the grounds (like the country of Finland does) would have prevented the damage. Is this what residents of the area—who lost family members, homes, businesses, and lands—wanted to hear from the President? Did anyone believe that the President was a fire expert from one conversation with the Finnish leader?

This wasn't a singular exhibition of outwardly insensitive behavior. When Hurricane Maria ravaged Puerto Rico in the Fall of 2017, Trump made the obligatory visit to San Juan to provide support and leadership. What do people remember from the event? The leader of our nation tossing paper towels to people—as if he was a king providing a ludicrous solution to everyone's problem. Paper towels became a symbolic version of "let them eat cake" (sometimes wrongly attributed to Marie Antoinette, bride of France's King Louis XVI circa 1789). Not only did video of his actions backfire, it depicted him as condescending and oafish.

Giving the President the benefit of the doubt, I do not believe he was being intentionally callus. Put simply, he is incapable of true empathy. I'm not excusing Trump's lack of skill in demonstrating empathy during times of crisis (such as his handling of the coronavirus epidemic, which we will discuss in Principle #3); I'm merely suggesting it's not in his DNA. Donald Trump was not, is not, and never will be a genuine people person. He said and did what he genuinely thought he was supposed to do in those aforementioned situations, and his actions missed the target. While this trait (or lack thereof) does not bother his base of ardent supporters, it repels millions of other people in the United States and abroad.

To be fair, few Presidents have been known for their ability to express empathy. Many of them—Washington, Grant, and Eisenhower, to name some obvious ones—were important military figures and were elected because of their honorable service to country and strategic experience from the battlefield, rather than their level of sensitivity.

Still, President Franklin Delano Roosevelt was able to unite America during the Depression and even into World War II with his unique ability to communicate with the people through his warm Fireside Chats. President Roosevelt's polio affliction made him a sympathetic figure in the eyes of American citizens; he seemed to truly understand the pain of America's poor and afflicted.

President Bill Clinton had an uncanny ability to rise to the occasion and demonstrate just the right amount of empathy as needed. Whether he was sincere or not may be inconsequential in the larger scheme of things; he helped people get through troubling times and eased much pain and suffering when he had to step up.

President Jimmy Carter showed visible pain and distress when people were suffering. A genuine humanitarian, Carter truly cares about people from all walks of life—and not just Americans. The question arises, however: *Can too much empathy ever become a bad thing?*

In Carter's case, I believe it was. His compassion was admirable, but it clouded his judgement in terms of issues such as national security and the economy.

More recently, President Barack Obama wore his empathy on his sleeve and occasionally called people out for lacking the trait. This may have alienated some people who thought he was condescending, though in a different way from his rival, President Trump.

The upshot is that we expect our civil servants to have at least a modicum of empathy and know when to turn it on, turn it off, and purport themselves well according to the circumstances at the time. It's a delicate balance. Our leaders must represent all of the people and at least convincingly pretend to care.

The one thing we do know for sure is that *in*sensitivity is *never* a desirable trait for one who holds office.

Maintains a Sense of Humor

Time for a quick quiz. Say the secret word and win $100. (Are you old enough to place this reference? The answer to this question—and the secret word—will be revealed before the next subheading, I promise.)

Identify which Presidents said the following quips:

A. *He can compress the most words into the smallest ideas better than any man I ever met.*

B. *I am not worried about the deficit. It is big enough to take care of itself.*

C. *All free governments are managed by the combined wisdom and folly of the people.*

D. *If I had to name my greatest strength, I guess it would be my humility. Greatest weakness, it's possible that I'm a little too awesome.*

E. *If you've got them by the balls, their hearts and minds will follow.*

F. *Mothers all want their sons to grow up to be President, but they don't want them to become politicians in the process.*

Any guesses on the above? All right, fine, I'll tell you.

A. President Lincoln

B. President Reagan

C. President Garfield

D. President Obama

E. President Theodore Roosevelt

F. President Kennedy

The above Presidential one-liners may not be worthy of standup comedian Henny Youngman (if you go back that far), but they are witty. They also reveal a great deal about the characters of each of the individuals:

- Lincoln: master of the verbal barb

- Reagan: ability to quell the nation's fears about a major issue

- Garfield: flippant about human nature and intellect

- Obama: confident enough to joke about himself

- Roosevelt: edgy!

- Kennedy: understood the pitfalls of high office

Some of you may be thinking: *All right, these men had (or, in Obama's case, have) a gift for expressing clever wordplay, raising a smile, and capturing a moment—but is humor really an essential attribute of a great leader?*

I assert *yes*: While humor is far from being the most important among my list of a dozen criteria, it most certainly deserves to be given its due. Allow me to explain why.

A sense of humor is essential for humans (and even monkeys, if you've ever been to the zoo). Making people smile is a gift: If you doubt my word on this, take a look at how many people were devastated by the passing of humorist Will Rogers a century ago and, more recently, Robin Williams in 2014. It takes immense talent, courage, and skill to make people laugh and comes naturally to precious few individuals. We admire and respect people who know how to tell a joke—and have a thick enough skin to be on the receiving end of one, as well. Being a good sport shows you are human, which often suggests *humility* (see the next attribute).

While in office, President Gerald Ford was captured on film more than once taking an embarrassing stumble. This did not escape the comedic lance of one Chevy Chase on *Saturday Night Live* TV show, who parodied the President's clumsiness with hilarious results. One could say Chase was disrespectful of the President and/or his office, but few ever voiced objection. In fact, the biggest fan of the sketches was none other than President Ford himself! Over the years, the two men met and developed something of a personal friendship.

By contrast, let's review Alec Baldwin's imitations of President Trump on *Saturday Night Live*, which began around 2016. How did the President react? Instead of coming back with something amusing, a self-deprecating joke, or even just letting it roll off his shoulders, Trump lashed out at the performer on Twitter as having a "mediocre career" that "was saved by his terrible impersonation of me."

Why did the President feel the need to dignify Baldwin and fight back? Why couldn't he have been more like Ford and been a good sport? Baldwin's imitation clearly got under his skin and bothered him. Like any other bully, he demonstrated that he could dish it out but couldn't take it. In my view, these are unsavory traits for any leader to have.

As demonstrated by President Reagan, a well-timed, well-worded joke in the proper hands could elicit smiles among the people—even when we are facing a crisis. Whether it was his acting skills coming into play is irrelevant. Reagan had a knack for being able to say funny things that made people feel at ease without seeming insensitive. In other words, since the President is able to gently joke about the issue, it must mean we will get through it and everything will be okay.

Unfortunately, there isn't any film of President Lincoln performing his standup act but, by all accounts, he was a magnificent joke-teller and had a marvelous quick and savage wit. (This ability was well represented by Daniel Day-Lewis in the 2012 film *Lincoln*.) Our sixteenth President was known to break up a bitter mood with a well-timed joke—but it was almost always to make a point. He could read a room well and would use his sense of humor to help convince people of his ideals and proposed actions.

Humor in the wrong hands, however, can be devastating. A leader should *never ever* use humor to deride, insult, bully, stereotype, embarrass, hurt, or alienate a fellow citizen (especially one who isn't a political rival). If you are laughing with a President who physically mocks an individual with a disability, you may wish to take some classes in Humor 101 and study the works of genuinely funny insult comics such as the Marx Brothers, Mel Brooks, Joan Rivers, and Don Rickles—all of whom knew the right targets to hit and wink at audiences to let them know not to take them too seriously.

So, where does the line, "Say the secret word and win $100" come from? If you answered Groucho Marx in the TV show *You Bet Your Life*, you would be correct! What do you win? The honor of finding out the secret word mentioned at the beginning of this section at no extra charge.

The secret word is *humility*, our very next attribute. After all, *humor* and *humility* go together hand in hand—or foot in foot.

It's apropos to end this section with a remark from comedian Groucho Marx that would also sound right coming from the lips of a politician: "Quote me as saying I was mis-quoted."

Demonstrates Humility

As I'm sure you've gathered by now, it takes quite a unique individual with a wide range of abilities to become a great leader. One of the most difficult aspects, perhaps, is to be a humble civil servant while at the same time maintaining a strong level of confidence. (We will get to the latter attribute soon enough.)

Put simply, one must be able to wield power in such a way that the ego is kept in check. Why is this so important for a political leader—especially the President? I may sound like a broken record, but it's all about *We the People*. Being the leader of the greatest nation in the free world means *working for the people*. As soon as a leader starts boasting about his or her accomplishments, it means he or she has submerged the American people while raising him or herself up to be an autocrat.

The United States hasn't had that many Presidents known for their humility. President Trump may the most egotistical of all Presidents, having bragged about his brain, his inauguration crowd size, his economy, being an environmental expert, a medical authority, and many other things that were clear-cut exaggerations, if not all-out falsehoods. In my opinion, braggadocio at this level is a sign of a person who is so insecure he feels he must create his own absurd fantasy version of the facts to prop himself up and feel good.

The obvious humble leaders who leap to mind are Presidents Washington and Lincoln. While we don't have the benefit of sound, video, or film of these great men, we do have the legacy of their words, writings, and accomplishments, as well as the observations about them from others.

As I previously mentioned, President Washington was both a reluctant leader and one who refused to take on the title of "king"; he would not accept a position that in any way, shape, or form hinted of "monarch." He also refused to wear his military uniform while serving as President, as he believed this would make him seem more important than other private citizens. During the Revolutionary War, there are countless examples of General Washington having been in the muddy trenches with his men during the harsh, cold winter months.

By nature, President Lincoln was a humble and reserved man who exhibited a great deal of perseverance. When he first ran for public office, he described himself as "young and unknown to many." As a leader, he hired people he considered best for the position—even if they had been insulting to him or posed threats. Edwin Stanton, one of his selections for Secretary of War, once referred to him as a "long-armed ape." Once in the position, Stanton continued to insult the President, repeatedly calling him a "damn fool." When Lincoln heard about this he reflected, "If Stanton said I was a damn fool, then I must be one, for he is nearly always right and generally says what he means."

The above paragons aside, one can also search outside America to find examples of humble leaders:

- Mark Rutte, the Prime Minister of the Netherlands, once spilled his coffee while entering the Ministry of Health. He mopped up the mess himself.

- Jose Mujica, the former President of Uruguay, donated all of his money to charity when he was elected to office and lived on a modest farm, instead of in the Presidential mansion.

- On one occasion, Canadian Prime Minister Justin Trudeau greeted Syrian refugees at the airport by presenting them with winter coats.

As Reverend Jesse Jackson said, "Never look down on anybody unless you're helping them up." I couldn't agree more.

Conveys Passion

The word *passion* has many different meanings, but in this instance, I want to emphasize that I am only referring to the leader as being passionate about the country. I have strong distaste for leaders with an abundance of passion for themselves, their political parties, and winning, but not so much for the United States as a whole.

Not only do I look for our nation's leaders to have unbridled, unconditional love for our nation, I expect that this translates to optimism and a bright future for everyone—not just the wealthy and privileged few. Presidents Reagan, Obama, and Clinton had a powerful ability to convey their passion for our country and citizens, and then make it exciting and contagious. People long to become part of something bigger. President Reagan's previously mentioned "Made in America" campaign generated a significant amount of passion during his terms of office.

We also need leaders who want to hold office and truly enjoy the job. President Theodore Roosevelt fits into this category, referring to the Presidency as the "Bully Pulpit." President John Quincy Adams' passion for the role comes across loud and clear in his elaborately detailed diary.

My experience in business is that employee performance dramatically improves when passionate leadership exists. People *want* to follow the leader and for the organization to succeed. This combined passion is enormously powerful and leads to tremendous results. Don't we want—and expect—the same for our country?

Exudes Confidence

It goes without saying that *confidence* is a requisite trait for leaders in both business and politics. More often than not, it's innate among those who seek leadership positions. Confident people assume they can handle a great deal of responsibility and believe they are deserving of high-level positions. In order to successfully move up the ranks in an organization, you must be able to deal with adversaries, weather any storm, and take some tough criticism—especially if you are in the public eye.

In terms of leadership, I believe confidence is distinct from courage, which is the next trait (and also Principle #4). In my mind, a confident leader must be poised and self-assured at all times without revealing what cards he or she is holding. As mentioned earlier, such confidence must be balanced with a certain amount of humility. Talk about difficult talents to master at the same time!

While political leadership in America has experienced something of a shortage of humbleness over the years, our civil servants have rarely lacked confidence. It requires a lot of belief in yourself to run for office in the first place and then stay the course, despite inevitable setbacks and failures. Once you get there, you need to constantly prove your worth, defend yourself against antagonism, push through your legislation, and face the press day in and day out. I don't mean to solicit sympathy for our politicians (I doubt they would get much, anyway!), but it is no easy task to be front and center, especially in the age of the Internet and social media.

At last, we have hit upon an area in which President Trump truly shines! Our forty-fifth President may, in fact, be the single most confident Commander-in-Chief we have ever had. Is this a strength or a weakness? His ardent followers would assert the former, whereas his naysayers would suggest that his excessive amount of confidence exposes areas in which he *lacks* confidence.

I don't pretend to be a political analyst or a psychologist (though I happen to have a Ph.D. in Psychology and Organizational Behavior), so I will simply put forth the idea that, despite the President's overwhelming exterior outer confidence, he is not to be upheld as emblematic of this trait. To many Americans and people around the world, his level of confidence is so over the top that it suggests the opposite about his psyche. A great leader should not feel the need to toot his own horn; instead, he or she should leave this up to the pundits and historians to decide.

When you think of a confident American leader, what image do you conjure? In my mind, I visualize General George Washington depicted in Emanuel Leutze's famous painting, *Washington Crossing the Delaware*: his chest held high as he proudly stands at the bow looking out toward the dangerous waters ahead. It's important to note that the boat is overloaded with war-weary colonial soldiers determined to navigate the icy waters. While many factual liberties were taken by the artist in the representation, the result is a portrait of confidence that is not about chest-beating, barking orders, or wielding power. Washington is supremely confident, in-charge, and among the people.

President Andrew Jackson, known as Old Hickory, was one of our most controversial Presidents. On the downside, many historians hold him accountable for having taken lands away from the Native American people and for supporting slavery. On the other hand, no one can doubt his level of confidence, especially when he was on the right side of history: he was the first President to exercise veto power; and he won re-election to a second term by battling what he considered to be the corrupt Second Bank of the United States.

Confidence, therefore, is a slippery slope. A leader must find a seamless balance between humility and courage. Whether in business or in politics, no one wants a leader at the top who is insecure, hesitant, or wishy-washy. A leader must convincingly stand by his or her convictions and also maintain enough confidence and sense of self to admit a mistake. Perhaps the most famous Presidential *mea culpa* dates back to 1961 when President John F. Kennedy took sole responsibility for the botched attempt to overthrow Cuban leader Fidel Castro in an incident that became known as the Bay of Pigs: "Victory has a hundred fathers, but defeat is an orphan... I am the responsible officer of the government." This became one of those rare moments when admitting a mistake actually *increased* a President's popularity. Human beings make mistakes and Kennedy made it clear that he did not consider himself an exception.

Confidence may appear in many forms, depending on the individual style of the leader. There isn't any one single route to take, as long as it doesn't cross over to hubris. Theodore Roosevelt and Franklin Delano Roosevelt may have shared the same last name, served as President, and presented themselves as confident leaders, but they couldn't have been any further apart in terms of personal style: the former was an action-taker who championed causes and seemed to thrive in battling for them; the latter was known for holding firm on his convictions, conquering an affliction (polio), and serving as a masterful orator. Peacemakers such as Mahatma Gandhi and Martin Luther King Jr. were amply confident in their beliefs and risked their lives for them. Business leaders such as Bill Gates and Steve Jobs were not imposing physical figures, yet they exuded an enormous amount of confidence while speaking about their respective businesses.

Most of all, the country feels safe and secure in the hands of a confident leader who can look a camera right in the eye to deliver a difficult message and be tough, stern, humorous, or inspirational as a situation dictates.

I can't think of any better way to end this section than the following quote from President Ronald Reagan: "Don't be afraid to see what you see."

Displays Courage

Take a wild guess who said the following: "There is no living thing that is not afraid when it faces danger. The True courage is in facing danger when you are afraid, and that kind of courage you have in plenty."

If you thought the quote came from a political leader or

a military hero, you would be mistaken. The lines, which appear within the pages of L. Frank Baum's story *The Wizard of Oz*, were uttered by Oz to the Cowardly Lion.

Whereas confidence is necessary all of the time, courage primarily becomes necessary when an individual is presented with dire circumstances, is taking a great risk, or must make a major sacrifice. We often label Presidents as courageous by thinking in terms of the times during which they held office: President Lincoln endured the Civil War; President Franklin Delano Roosevelt led during the Depression and World War II; and Kennedy dealt with the Cold War. Presidents who served during relatively peaceful times by comparison were fortunate enough to not have had their courage tested in such stressful times.

Military personnel must face off against seen and unseen danger all of the time—and not just in battle. Soldiers are often required to do things such as parachute from aircraft in dangerous weather conditions and test volatile machinery and weaponry. All of these things require immense bravery, which we often take for granted because our dedicated military men and women are trained to perform their duties as second nature and without fanfare.

Business leaders aren't exactly risking life and limb in their corner offices, but they must conquer a realm of potential threats—from competition to poor market conditions—and frequently make decisions on-the-spot that impact the fate of their organizations and people. Certainly, a corporate executive making a presentation to the Board of Directors is going to have butterflies in her stomach, as is the CEO signing off on a $10 million acquisition.

We will explore courage in politics at length in Principle #4 but, at present, let's address the subject only in terms of being a leadership attribute. The American people evidently believe that courage is an admirable and important trait, as more than half of our Presidents (58%, to be exact) served in the military. Voters realize that, during terms of conflict and global threats, a commander-in-chief with military experience can be valuable. The theory is that a veteran would best relate to our brave soldiers and have important insights into knowing when to send troops, retreat, or negotiate peace.

President Washington had unequivocally demonstrated his leadership skills and courage on the field of battle. He is the perfect example of a strategist who knew how to protect his army, learn from his mistakes, and play the long game to achieve victory against the dominating British forces. As our most important general during the Revolutionary War, he had the whole package; his courage, confidence, and humility earned the trust and respect of soldiers, politicians, and citizens alike. When he became President, he had the courage to recognize that the country needed to settle down with its own government before getting embroiled in another conflict.

President Ulysses S. Grant serves as a unique case study. A brilliant general, he led the Union to victory in numerous Civil War battles. As often happens with courageous military leaders, he was accustomed to taking calculated risks and had no issue disagreeing with his fellow officers. Whereas many generals believed the road to victory would only be achieved by winning territory, General Grant stuck to his convictions and focused more on defeating the Confederate army; his approach prevailed, and the Union won the war.

Although he had no political experience whatsoever, General Grant was elected as the eighteenth President of the United States. The natural theory was that a heroic leader on the battlefield was more than enough qualification to run the nation. Although he worked hard to repair wounds left by the Civil War and further the cause of equality for African Americans, he could not maintain order in an administration that was riddled with corruption. History has shown that, while he exemplified courage on the battlefield, he froze when it came to defeating his dangerous political rivals.

President Kennedy is noted for having literally written the book on this subject: *Profiles in Courage*. Interestingly, his work focused on *political* courage—not military. Kennedy chose to examine the courageous political accomplishments of eight senators who boldly went up against their own parties and supporters to do what they thought was right, at great risk to their own positions. Evidently, Kennedy was well aware of the importance of this leadership attribute and found inspiration from other brave politicians who had preceded him. We will look at some these men—both known and lesser-known—and why Kennedy selected them in Principle #4.

For now, I will leave you with this timeless quote from *Profiles in Courage*: "A man does what he must—in spite of personal consequences, in spite of obstacles and dangers, and pressures—and that is the basis of all human morality."

Radiates Style

At long last, we have reached the twelfth leadership attribute: radiates style.

Does inclusion of style mean to suggest that icons of past and present—i.e., Cary Grant, Fred Astaire, Audrey Hepburn, Elizabeth Taylor, Madonna, or Lady Gaga—would make suitable political leaders? Of course not. But I do believe our leaders should have style and class that befits their titles. In particular, the person who sits in the Oval Office must present him or herself with proper decorum that is inviting, dignified, and best represents our country at that time.

Leadership style—whether in business or politics—refers to both the manner in which you direct others, as well as how you look and behave. Some great leaders are determined and aggressive; others are more low-key, casual, and personal. Much of this has to do with the individual's personality and what type of leader is needed at the time he or she is in office.

Developing a unique individual style is important in order for the people to know how to accurately interpret what he or she says and does. There is no right or wrong here, as long as the leader is able to carry off the style, communicates well, has strong character, and effectively serves the people.

Some people are born with style, while others must be groomed. For the President of the United States, style means purporting oneself well on the world's stage at all times. This is essential for handling meetings with foreign dignitaries; respecting people from other cultures; and displaying class, manners, and respect to Americans from all types of backgrounds. A President must also be well-prepared and well-versed on clothing, etiquette, gestures, behaviors, and conversation in order to strengthen relationships with allies and negotiate with adversaries.

You don't have to be an editor at *GQ* to recognize from photographs alone that Presidents Kennedy, Clinton, and Obama all excelled in terms of stylish presentation and used this as an asset. Past generations would attest to Presidents Chester Arthur and Harry Truman as also having been pretty snazzy fellows.

The First Families matter, too. The Kennedys and Obamas were stylish trendsetters—especially First Lady Jackie Kennedy, who famously invited the viewers for a tour of the White House on television in grand style. During this time, Americans looked up to the First Family as style icons, which created a certain sense of national pride.

Of course, there is always the cliché "clothes don't make the man." Wherever possible, we need Presidents who look and act the part and are able to treat others with respect. A slob and a slouch don't cut it for most people. The following Presidents fell short in this area:

- President Lyndon Johnson: known to be vulgar

- John Adams: rude to people to the point of losing support

- James Monroe: threw temper tantrums

- John Quincy Adams: often described as "aloof, stubborn, and ferociously independent"

- Andrew Jackson: so stubborn that the Democratic party's symbol became the donkey

And now, at present, we have a leader (hint: he wears a red tie) who lies and boasts while insulting anyone and everyone who disagrees with him, whether political rival or not. His attitude has always been to "punch back," which is admired by his base of followers at his political rallies but is considered crass by members of the other party.

We can attempt to overlook a lot of this, but not when it comes to how he represents our country on the world's stage. He praised a congressman who body-slammed a reporter; attacked journalists for asking questions he dislikes; referred to certain places from where immigrants originate as "shithole countries"; described white nationalists as being "very fine people"; stepped in the rain holding an umbrella for himself but not for his wife, the First Lady; rudely pranced in front of the Queen of England during a ceremony; shoved the leader of Montenegro to get in front of him; and…oh my goodness, I must stop! In the words of film star and martial arts expert Bruce Lee: "Knowledge will give you power, but character respect."

To close this rather lengthy chapter on leadership attributes, I think it is important to reiterate that it is not any one of these characteristics that determines who will serve as a great leader. Few individuals are capable of pulling off the complete dozen at the same time, nor is this even necessary. Not everyone can be as gifted as Presidents Washington, Lincoln, Kennedy, and Reagan at so many things, since it is rare to find people who maintain these abilities and also be interested in pursuing the Presidency. At a minimum, however, we must expect that the President of the United States can excel at these attributes as the situations call for them.

In Principle #3 we are going to unpack an area in which America can stand the greatest amount of improvement: truth-telling. We have arrived at a place where it has become impossible to trust the government and the media. But we have the power to elect more trustworthy officials, hold the press accountable for accurate reporting, and be more educated and discerning in terms of what we believe.

We have a choice: *America the fantasy* or *America the beautiful*. I much prefer the latter.

PRINCIPLE #3: *Truth-Seeking*

If you ever injected truth in politics, you would have no politics.

—*Will Rogers, humorist*

What does *truth-seeking* mean in the world of politics? Is such a thing even possible?

With such pervasiveness of lies, distortions, and exaggerations overwhelming our political landscape, one wonders if the phrase "truth, justice, and the American way" means anything anymore. Is the American Dream complete fiction, like Superman?

Let's give our politicians the benefit of the doubt. In previous chapters, I made the case that there are occasions when politicians must lie in order to protect our national security. There are also circumstances when telling the truth might be positively ruinous for a Presidential administration and/or political party and, I suppose, they don't see any way around it.

However, while it is understandable why this happens on a daily basis in American politics, I cannot in good conscience condone lying. Why? Country *always* comes first over both personal interests and the needs of the party. Any political leader who does otherwise should be drummed right out of office.

Let's take a look at what usually happens in business. If you are a CEO, President, or member of a Board of Directors in a corporate organization and are caught in a lie, what do you think occurs? There is an investigation, followed by a vote. Unless the entire organization is corrupt and heading down the tubes (such as Enron), there aren't any politics or coverups involved. If the evidence of the lie is incontrovertible, that individual is escorted out the door with a box of his or her possessions and a plant. No one wants to get dragged into someone else's lie that might potentially tarnish his or her reputation or possibly even risk jail time. These days, the lie is often associated with one of two things: financial malfeasance or sexual impropriety. In the case of the former: If the business leader is stuffing his or her pockets with company money, guess who loses out? *The Board members. The other leaders. The shareholders. The company's partners. The customers who pay their hard-earned money for the product or service.* In the case of the latter: The pendulum has tilted in the complete opposite direction, and companies will not take risk when it comes to anything smacking of sexual misconduct.

Most importantly, in both circumstances, let's not forget the employees. What did all of these dedicated people do to deserve suffering the loss of earnings and damage to their reputations by working for a company with a leader who lies and cheats or harasses coworkers?

Simply put, we do not hold our politicians up to the same moral and ethical standard as individuals in our business community. They get away with too much because we allow them to do so. We look the other way when a politician lies and commits a wrongdoing because we like his or her agenda. Or, we give a free pass because we think the politician is good for the economy, which means our stocks are soaring and our wallets fully stuffed.

What is wrong with this picture? Everything.

In my view, this is hypocritical. If business leaders must be held accountable, so should our political leaders. Lying has been considered the "norm" in politics for too long because the politicians believe they are invulnerable, and all too often we allow them to slide through out of our own greed or political interests in the politician's agenda. This must stop!

Of course, politicians are not the only guilty parties. Newspapers and television networks have also been miscommunicating, distorting, and/or withholding information as well. When you can't trust either the people in charge or the media reporting on them, you have a banana republic.

Well, let's start peeling that banana and cut straight to the truth.

LIARS-IN-CHIEF

Sadly, with few exceptions, American Presidents have had a difficult time with the truth, including a few of those I praised in the previous chapter as having demonstrated several virtuous leadership abilities. Alas, no one is perfect. Such is the tragedy when it comes to Presidential power, the pressures of the oval office, constant public scrutiny, and human weakness. President John F. Kennedy—whom many considered a beacon of dignity, honesty, and class— lied about myriad things to the American public: his suffering from Addison's disease; his gangster connections; and his extra-marital affairs with movie stars and other women. President Bill Clinton was impeached not for his improper relationship with intern Monica Lewinsky, but for having lied under oath about it. President Richard Nixon not only denied having had anything to do with the Watergate break-in, he went to great lengths to lie about it and cover it up.

There really is no escaping the fact that Presidents have a hard time with the truth. "Spin" is one thing, but a bold-face lie is another. And yes, the volume, degree, and context of the lying does matter quite a bit. As a case in point,

The Washington Post reported that President Donald Trump made over 15,413 false claims in his first three years in office. That's an average of *fifteen public fibs per day*!

You may be able to excuse or not care about Trump's lies about the size of his inauguration crowd and whether or not he had relations with a porn star and paid her off with campaign funds to remain silent. But what happens when he lies about Russian interference in the 2016 election? Where does the line get crossed?

I'll tell you when. Any Presidential lie is bad, but the worst instance is when our Democracy is being threatened. Despite statements from every major American government agency that Russia had meddled in our election, President Trump denied and/or downplayed this fact at every turn. To date, he still hasn't admitted that it was Russia who did it. I don't care whether the President is best buds with Putin; or Putin duped or pressured him into refuting Russian interference; or that he was covering up his campaign's involvement in the scandal; or that he simply didn't want his election victory to be tainted. We may never fully understand his motivations. But, if we cannot trust the results of our elections, we are once again back to turning into a banana republic. Worse, we are puppets of a foreign power and a laughingstock on the world's stage.

As I stated in the previous chapter, the President needs to purport himself (or herself, which will happen at some point in our history, I'm sure) well at all times. He is the Commander-in-Chief and representative of our country as a whole. What does chronic lying say to the business community—that it's okay to do if you have support of the people around you (i.e., the Senate)? What does it tell our children—that you can lie all you want if you wield enough power?

The Trump Presidency reached an all-time low when it came to the Ukraine scandal that led to his being impeached by the House of Representatives. As attested by numerous credible witnesses—lifelong diplomats and service people from both sides of the aisle—the President attempted to pressure the newly elected Ukrainian President Volodymyr Zelensky by withholding approved military aid in exchange for dirt on his political rival, former Vice President Joe Biden. The snowstorm of lies, backpedaling, and cover-ups culminated with the Republican Senate dropping the whole thing without even calling witnesses, in order to protect the President. Only one Republican Senator, Mitt Romney, stood apart from his fellow senators and voted against the President. Once again, the President's bad behavior was given a free pass and he felt entitled enough by the outcome to announce his own vindication.

Some of you may be upset, if not downright angry, while reading the previous paragraphs. (I can only imagine the rancor forthcoming in Twitter feeds!) Perhaps you believe everything the President did was perfectly copacetic. Or, you may believe the President lied and should know better than to do a quid pro quo with a foreign government, but do not feel it's an impeachable offense. The theory goes like this: The Democrats had it out for the President from the very beginning and made up the whole scandal or are blowing it out of proportion. Well, you are entitled to your opinion, which is what makes America great!

I, for one, believe the entire scandal was corrosive and our leaders should be ashamed of themselves for allowing the President to wheel and deal at the expense of our allies and our nation's integrity. History will not look favorably upon these individuals who chose party and agenda above what was true and just. But that isn't even the worst of what is happening in our era. Let's look at the real dangers when human lives are at stake…

WHEN LYING BECAME ENDEMIC WITH AN EPIDEMIC

In early 2020, while this work was being researched and written, the world was caught off-guard by something of a black swan, an emerging new contagion: *coronavirus* (COV1D-19). It is believed to have begun in Wuhon, China in December 2019 and then spread throughout Asia and Europe. The first cases of the disease in America materialized in February 2020. The global impact has been catastrophic: thousands of lives lost; people stuck in quarantines and sickbeds; businesses drawn to a screeching halt; and financial markets plummeting.

A global health crisis is by no means an easy time for any President. It's also not the first occasion in recent memory when a President had to deal with a major health crisis: President Obama had to deal with both swine flu *and* ebola during his terms.

For the sake of humanity, I truly hope that President Trump, all global leaders, and the health community at large can quell this issue with minimal pain, suffering, and lives lost. The cost to our economy and wallets is painful, indeed, but secondary.

Recognizing that the markets were starting to go south, President Trump attempted to get ahead of the panic and held a press conference. It was the right thing to do, especially since the American people demanded assurances that the spread of the contagion was being contained, testing was widely available, and a cure was urgently being sought. This was a time that called for *transparency*. The American people wanted truthful answers to these urgent questions: *What should the American people expect? What should we be afraid of? What precautions should we take? What are the genuine risks? Is it safe to travel?*

Unfortunately, things did not go well out of the gate. Instead of rising to the occasion and doing what was right and best for the American people, President Trump lied…and lied…and lied. Presumably, he wanted to show he had things well under control, was doing a great job, and there was no need to worry. Why? Because he was concerned about the plummeting stock market and its impact on his re-election bid, his own pockets, and his fragile ego having to withstand criticism.

These are just a few of the lies and misstatements:

- **Lie:** In the United States, the number of cases is "going very substantially down, not up."

Fact: The CDC (the Center for Disease Control) made it clear that the exact opposite was going to occur.

- **Misstatement:** He stated that we are "rapidly developing a vaccine…and will essentially have a flu shot for this in a fairly quick manner."

Fact: A spokesperson for the National Institute of Allergy and Infectious Diseases reported that a vaccine won't be ready for at least "a year to a year-and-a-half." Can this time frame really be considered a "fairly quick manner"?

- **Misstatement *and* Lie:** Regarding the fifteen cases in America reported, he said, "the fifteen, within a couple of days, is going to be down to close to zero. That's a pretty good job we've done."

Fact: There is no possible way for the number of cases to "go down to zero." Once the cases are counted (i.e., the fifteen), they are always part of the tally—even if the individuals fully recover (which could not have been known by the President at that time). The CDC and other health organizations did not concur with the President's assessment that the number would go down. Roughly one week after the President's ill-advised statements, the number of cases in the U.S. soared to well over 100 across sixteen states. (At this point in time, the number is rapidly approaching a million.)

I don't care whether you are a Republican or Democrat, *the truth matters*—especially when it comes to a health crisis. By consistently lying and downplaying the numbers and severity of the outbreak, lives—American and global—are placed at risk.

Let me make it perfectly clear: A President should be calm and confident during a time like this. President Trump accomplished that in spades. But if we can't trust that he is telling the truth, we will not know whether we: can safely travel on an airplane, train, bus or subway; are at risk if we are of a certain age; need to wear masks in public or not; can send our kids to school; and so forth. I am not exaggerating by this statement: *In times such as these, lives are at stake and people demand and deserve the truth.*

Instead, President Donald Trump suggested that the new coronavirus would "go away" in April, as temperatures warm. This was completely unsubstantiated and unproven and, in fact, downright dangerous. Does this mean the scientific community should have stopped looking for a cure because the virus would dissipate on its own?

The best thing any President can do in such a challenging situation is leave the announcements and facts up to the proven medical community, not to himself or loyalist lackeys who might misreport information to make the President look and feel good. The President needs to stay on script and not exaggerate or make stuff up for the sake of protecting his own interests. Instead, he should say something to the effect of, "Everyone is working around the clock to contain the contagion, find a cure, and protect everyone. The medical community advises that the best thing you can do is wash your hands properly and avoid putting your hands to your face—your nose, eyes, and mouth—since that is how the disease gets into your system."

There may be those readers who unconditionally love the President and therefore cannot and will not be convinced of the severity of the lying issue. You may, in fact, hold the extremist view that the Democrats made up the coronavirus to hurt the President or are somehow blaming him for worsening the crisis. You may even be among those who agree with President Trump's original assertions that the virus is "fake news" and go as far as protesting the business shutdowns without adhering to social distancing guidelines provided by the medical community.

Please: Let's be rational and choose not to go to any of those places. The main overarching concern is that politicians and citizens must face the truth, even when it might be something they don't like to hear or might hurt their chances of re-election, retaining their jobs, or improving the stock market and the economy. The safety and welfare of our people are always more important than accruing wealth and power…aren't they?

Whether you are rich or poor, young or old, Republican or Democrat, no one is 100% immune to the COVID-19 or any other mass epidemic. (You may be a carrier and not even realize it.) Let's ensure all Americans are healthy, wise, and educated so we may overcome the desperate times as a united force—and later, when we come through it, we can enjoy the prosperous ones together.

FAKE NEWS HAS BECOME OUR REALITY

As I indicated earlier in this chapter, communication outlets have also become untrustworthy. Major national newspapers now must compete against the digital universe of the Internet and social media for reportage. Everyone wants the "scoop," and a blog or social media platform has an immediacy to reach millions of people that old school newspapers simply can't compete against. In the race to be the first to report a piece of information, tabloid headlines become viral and presumed to be fact. Photos and videos can be doctored by a twelve-year-old. But where is the fact-checking and honesty? In light of Russian interference in the 2016 election, how do we know the actual source of reported information and whether it can be trusted?

All of these issues become exacerbated in the world of politics. Many people are fine with spreading misinformation about a politician on the other side of the aisle, whether they believe it or not. During President Obama's presidential run and thereafter, he was accused of not being a natural-born citizen (i.e., birther theory) and even of being a terrorist! People believed these lies because some individuals, such as future President Donald Trump (on his Twitter feed), and news sources, such as Breitbart and Fox News, wanted others to accept them to be true. Well, say what you want about President Obama's political agenda—and I disagreed with him on many things— he served two terms in office without a single tie to any terrorist activity or scandal. One might think that, if the birther theory and/or the terrorist accusations had been true, our country would have been exposed to *something* harmful during those eight years. We were not.

During the 2016 Presidential election, Democratic candidate Hillary Clinton was accused of many preposterous things. Perhaps the most absurd became known as "Pizzagate." On the air, Conservative radio show host Alex Jones reported that Clinton was sexually abusing children and performing Satanic rituals in the basement of Comet Ping Pong restaurant in Washington, D.C. Sounds preposterous, right? Again, you may not like Hillary Clinton or her politics, but a pedophile ring in a pizza parlor basement? Come on, people!

Well, there are real dangers to such outrageous reportage. Edgar Maddison Welch believed the propaganda and trekked all of the way from Salisbury, North Carolina to Washington, D.C. with an AR-15 semiautomatic rifle, a .38 handgun, and a folding knife. He burst into Comet Ping Pong, flung open a door, and found…cooking supplies. Oh, my goodness—summon the FBI! The pizza establishment *didn't even have a basement*, much less devote space to a child porn ring.

My point in recounting this story is to underscore the fact that bad journalism is as much of an issue as bad politics. People are trained to believe their news source at face value, whether it's Fox News, CNN, *The New York Times*, Breitbart, MSNBC, or a YouTube video from a ten-year-old in Dubuque, Iowa. Political propaganda now comes in all forms—including Russian bots—and there are millions of people out there who are gullible enough to believe whatever garbage is circulating. We know we are in trouble when we can't distinguish between honest news sources and Russian bots. Why do we wish to help Russia tear us apart?

Of course, news outlets make mistakes; they are run and owned by humans, of course. At the same time, biases do exist. *The New York Times*, to be sure, has an anti-Trump stance and printed emotionally charged headlines on several occasions (such as "Trump Blames Democrats for His

Separation Tactic") that had a grain of truth but were not completely objective in tone.

Then there is the counterattack. In response to articles he does not like, President Trump has sued publications and news networks (without a favorable result) and frequently accused them of "Fake News." It strikes me as amusing that the President has taken credit for coining the term *fake news*, which in of itself is fake news! It's unknown who first said it, but it is pretty evident it was not President Trump. Before he used the expression, it had already been popularized by Buzzfeed editor Craig Silverman.

So. *What about a certain Conservative news network that shall remain nameless?,* you may ask. I have a big problem with a television news outlet that manipulates the facts to brainwash its viewers, present opinions as fact, and prop up its party of choice. I take even greater issue with one that implants messages in the President's brain on a daily basis to impact major national decisions. Unfortunately, as long as there are ratings to be had and political landscapes to manipulate, I do not see any change happening on this front anytime soon.

However, I do believe there is something we can do to counter their efforts: The American people must unite as *truth-seekers*.

Wouldn't it be refreshing to see the following:

- A news channel praise a politician on the other side of the political aisle who made a good decision

- A news channel call out a politician on their side of the aisle for lying

- A politician come clean about a lie and then make up for it

- A media outlet catch a lie and make a conscious decision not to spread it as fact

- Twenty-four hours without someone in politics or the media lying

At the end of the day, it is up to us—*all Americans*—to question, probe, and be skeptical with regard to what we are being told. Let's make a vow to become truth-seekers and hold the people who create the news and those who report it accountable for accurate communication. If we can come together on this front, politicians and media people will no longer have a reason to lie and, in fact, might be afraid to do so at great risk of losing support.

In the beginning of this Principle, I cited the famous words generally associated with Superman: "truth, justice, and the American way." As most of us are aware, Clark Kent, his mild-mannered alter ego, happened to be a news reporter. Well, all of us—including politicians and media personnel—can strive to be supermen and superwomen, even though we are merely human: We have the power and ability to be *truth-seekers*.

All it takes is a little courage—which is precisely what the next Principle is all about.

PRINCIPLE #4: *Courage*

*It often requires more courage to dare
to do right than to fear doing wrong.*

—Abraham Lincoln, 16th President of the United States

You will recall that I previously covered *courage* as leadership attribute #11 back in Principle #2. Here we going to approach this subject on an everyday, individual level related to politics and what this looks like when a person is confronted by extreme pressure to do something that he or she knows is wrong.

For a portion of my leadership workshops, I like to screen films such as the following: *Twelve Angry Men, Twelve O'Clock High, Apollo 13, 127 Hours,* and *United 93.* What do you suppose these movies all have in common? If you were to answer, "They all have numbers in them," you would be 100% correct! In addition, I would suggest that they all dramatize human courage in powerful ways that may be applied to politics, as well as to business and other areas of life.

Let's break these films down a bit:

- *Twelve Angry Men*: Henry Fonda, as Juror #8, pushes back against eleven men who are convinced they should convict an inner-city teen accused of murder.

- *Twelve O'Clock High:* Gregory Peck stars as U.S. Air Force General Savage, who institutes tough policies with his men that are unpopular—until they realize that his harsh methods will toughen them up and keep them alive.

- *Apollo 13*: American astronauts heading to the moon experience numerous life-threatening technical issues and must improvise seemingly impossible solutions in order to survive and successfully return to earth.

- *127 Hours:* James Franco plays Aron Ralston, a mountaineer who gets trapped alone in a mountain with a boulder pinning his arm down.

- *United 93:* Dramatization of the real-life passengers aboard hijacked United Flight 93 on 9/11 as they react to their fate.

The above scenarios are all wildly different, yet they share a similar concept: The characters depicted are regular people who are placed in volatile situations and must find inner courage in order to defeat adversity. The challenges may involve societal prejudice (*Twelve Angry Men*), psychological frailty (*Twelve O'Clock High*), technology (*Apollo 13*), nature (*127 Hours*), or terrorism (*United 93*), but the theme of overcoming fear is prevalent in each circumstance. Additionally, human lives hang in the balance, so the stakes are astronomically high. (In *Twelve Angry Men*, this is the case concerning the fate of the young man on trial for murder.)

If you were to find yourself in a dire situation in which your life—or that of others—was being jeopardized because of a decision you make, how would you fare? Would you be able to rise to the occasion? It's easy to point a finger and judge when characters flicker on a movie screen. But what would you do if your courage were to be tested in actuality?

Some food for thought: *Apollo 13, 127 Hours*, and *United 93* were all based on real people who faced chilling, life-threatening threats. We happen to know how these individuals fared in their respective circumstances. In the first two films, the heroes survived. Though the passengers on Flight 93 were less fortunate, we do know that their efforts were at least successful in terms of preventing much greater human loss.

Dear reader, I truly hope these situations do not ever happen to you or to any of your loved ones. The truth of the matter, unfortunately, is that we face a variety of threats every single day. It may not involve being shot at while inside a bomber aircraft or being hopelessly trapped and bleeding to death in a mountain crevice, but even ordinary citizens occasionally get placed in harm's way and end up being forced to make critical decisions with lives hanging in the balance.

One of my favorite films (which, alas, does not have a number in the title) is *Saving Private Ryan*. In one scene, Captain Miller (portrayed by Tom Hanks)—the brave commanding officer—stuns his men (and the audience) when he reveals that he is merely an English teacher and not a career soldier or anything that traditionally requires so-called "bravery." He could be *any one of us*, which is what makes that film so charged and powerful.

I do not mean to trivialize this subject by referencing so many motion pictures. Rather, I use them to elucidate the point that a test of bravery might come at any one of us at any point in time and these particular films reflect this while also tugging on emotional strings. American history teems with examples of heroism from regular people rising to the occasion: from our volunteer patriots during the Revolutionary War (who were mainly boys); to the Greatest Generation of soldiers during World War II; to the brave fighting men and women of the conflicts in Korea and Vietnam; to the warriors around the globe who face continuing threats in Afghanistan and elsewhere in present-day. There are also instances of bravery—both seen and unseen—displayed by our officers, firefighters, and other public servants every single day of the year.

Although they aren't usually risking their lives, business-people must summon up courage as they make decisions that impact the livelihoods of dozens, hundreds, or perhaps even thousands of people. For example, as this is being written, COVID-19 is spreading throughout the world like wildfire. Across the board, leaders are making judgment calls with regard to whether schools should remain open; stadiums at sporting events and concert halls should be filled; employees should work from home or not; and so forth. These are not easy decisions to make! No one wishes to cause unnecessary hysteria or panic; on the other hand, people want to be smart about limiting the spread of this highly contagious—and potentially fatal—disease.

In the business world, it takes a certain amount of courage to make everyday decisions: hiring and firing; investing in another company or selling off a business; spending $1 million on a network upgrade; recalling a major order because one product was returned as defective; etc. You don't necessarily have to be an executive to demonstrate courage in business: You could be the whistleblower on a product defect that results in a recall which saves lives—but may cost the company a lot of money. Or, maybe you are the one who disagrees with a decision made by the CEO that would be disastrous, if you were to remain silent.

CAVING TO POLITICAL PRESSURE

In politics, what does courage look and feel like? Does it resemble anything like Jimmy Stewart as the naïve title character in *Mr. Smith Goes to Washington,* who must battle corrupt, powerful foes? Well, *sort of*—albeit in dramatic fashion. When Mr. Smith defends himself hour after hour with a filibuster in a desperate attempt to expose the truth (not to mention restore his soiled reputation) to the Senate and to the country, we feel every ounce of his pain and torture as he struggles to remain standing upright and continue to speak through his tortured voice.

As *Mr. Smith Goes to Washington* demonstrates, it requires enormous individual political courage to stand up in politics against overwhelming forces. In February 2020, *only one Republican* broke with the party to convict President Donald Trump of high crimes and misdemeanors: Utah Senator Mitt Romney. Was he doing it because he felt the evidence was conclusive and President Trump should be removed from office? Did he believe that if the President were to get away with such acts it would set harmful precedents? Or, was he responding to the moral judgments of his Mormon constituents in Utah? We'll never know which was the case and, in fact, the truth might reside somewhere in the middle. Either way, it took toughness and courage to go up against fifty-two senators—not to mention the President, his administration, Republican members of the House, and millions of Trump supporters—and vote "guilty." He voted in favor of only one of the two charges (abuse of power), but nevertheless, it was a bold and risky move by the Senator.

And yet…how do we feel about the rest of the Republican Party—both in the House and the Senate—who either defended the President's bad behavior or caved to the pressure and looked the other way? I'm not suggesting that the President's actions were necessarily at the level warranting him being ousted—that is a debate for another time—I'm merely presenting the case that, Romney aside, not one individual had the backbone to stand up for American values, principles, and our Constitution. Going back to our last Principle: The truth was blocked. We were never given a chance to hear from several key witnesses who would have revealed more about what happened among the President, his administration, and the Ukraine with regard to withholding military aid in exchange for dirt on Vice President Biden. Whether the facts support the President or not, don't the American people deserve to know the truth? Isn't having the courage to disclose and protect the truth a vital aspect of what we should demand and expect from our leaders?

Since President Trump's induction as President, numerous Republican officials (such as Senators Paul Ryan, Jeff Flake, and Bob Corker) have stepped down, caved to political pressure, sided with him on everything (Senator Mitch McConnell), or done a 180-degree turn-around and become a Trumpian puppet (Senator Lindsey Graham). At a time when the country most needed non-partisan leadership, there was not a single member of the GOP (Romney aside) who stood up and did what was in the best interests of our country. They failed to defend our Constitution and hold our President accountable in any way. If anything, by letting him get off scot-free, they empowered him to do whatever he wants including, potentially, welcome additional meddling in upcoming elections to help his re-election bid.

Why did so many of these Republicans buckle? Pure and simple: *fear.* They were afraid the President would Tweet something negative about them and/or likely turn the party against them. This seemed all too easy for Trump to accomplish. With one Tweet, he could make a patriot who served in our government seem "disloyal" for telling the truth under oath, and then turn his base against that individual. This actually occurred in one notable case with Lt. Col. Vindman, who was removed from his post after the Senate Impeachment trial ended. (Even Vindman's brother, Lieutenant Colonel Yevgeny Vindman, was given the boot—and he had nothing whatsoever to do with the Impeachment hearings.)

Should the Lt. Colonel have lied under oath to protect the President? *No.* Should he have been penalized for his honesty? An emphatic *No.*

I do not mean to get into the weeds opening up the window for a dispute on contemporary politics or whether you supported the Impeachment trial of #45 or not. Rather, my intention is to demonstrate that having an iron backbone is essential for our government to function properly. If our politicians don't have the courage to stand behind their principles when the shining moment arises, when will they ever do so? Given this, how can we ever trust politicians to be brave enough to have the backs of American citizens when we need them most?

All right…it's time for me to hop off my soap box, head in the opposite direction, and illustrate some fine examples of political courage throughout our history. It was a certain Senator and future President who helped shine a light on these courageous men, whose acts would otherwise have likely faded into history.

WHAT DOES TRUE POLITICAL COURAGE LOOK LIKE?

In 1955, President John F. Kennedy (then Senator Kennedy) wrote the Pulitzer Prize-winning book *Profiles in Courage.* Instead of profiling obvious types of heroes, such as soldiers, he chose to focus on eight American senators—some names familiar, some not—who demonstrated political courage of the highest order: John Quincy Adams, Daniel Webster, Thomas Hart Benton, Sam Houston, Edmund G. Ross, Lucius Lamar, Greg Norris, and Robert A. Taft.

Why were these eight selected? Because they had the

courage to stand up against their own party—as well as their own base—to do what they believed was right. Whether they had a certain ethical or moral streak, or simply desired to be on the right side of history, is beside the point; they put themselves out there at great risk to their offices, careers, reputations, and livelihoods.

Before he became the sixth President of the United States, John Quincy Adams was a Federalist Senator from Massachusetts. At various turns, Senator Adams voted contrary to his party's position, including his support of the Louisiana Purchase. Later, Adams again opposed his own party by siding with Thomas Jefferson to embargo British ships in retaliation against their various aggressions. Adams paid a steep price for sticking to his unpopular convictions, stepping down from his Senate position in 1808. He had the last laugh, however, winning the Presidency in 1825.

Ask yourself this question: In recent memory, has any Senator in either party outside Mitt Romney taken an extreme, unpopular chance like Senator Adams? The answer would be an obvious *No*.

Let's refer back to Kennedy's book for a lesser-known example, which happens to sound eerily contemporary. President Andrew Johnson, the 17th President of the United States, assumed office after Lincoln's assassination. While Johnson is now often regarded as one of America's worst Presidents for having clung to several historically bad positions (such as opposing African American rights), he became victim of a senatorial mob that wanted him removed from office without a fair Impeachment trial. Although he didn't care for Johnson, Kansas Senator Edmund Ross emphatically objected to the proceedings, believing that partisan politics shouldn't determine the fate of a President—especially without presentation of proper evidence. Senator Ross received a great deal of flack for his stance; not only did he lose his re-election bid, his family suffered massive abuse and were driven to poverty status. Fortunately, Ross was vindicated by the Supreme Court, albeit several years later.

The point here is that, while you don't have to like the President or agree with any of his positions, you can't stack the government against him. If that were to occur, any political gang could tip the balance of government power to suit its fancy without a proper hearing. Senator Ross may have lost the battle but, ultimately, won the war. He stuck to his guns and chose the big picture of his country above party needs and his personal likes and dislikes.

Surely, we could use a man like Ross in the Senate right now!

COURAGE IS INTEGRAL TO CHARACTER

During President Reagan's presidency, the Republican platform stood for things such as Democratic capitalism, fiscal conservatism, traditional social order, and strong national defense. While I understand that times change and a party can evolve, I believe—as do many traditional Republicans—that the GOP has gone far off-course and is barely recognizable. One of the guiding ideas of Republicanism, for example, had been the reduction of government spending. As of this writing, the U.S. national debt is at $24.2 trillion and soaring.

Why don't the Republicans in the House and the Senate seem to care about this? It's entirely possible many do—and yet they have chosen to remain silent. In my view, this reflects the state of affairs of when it comes to assessing the character of our politicians today. Truth-seeking and courage are two sides of this coin; you cannot have one without the other and consider yourself to have *character*. If, for example, you wholeheartedly buy into a party's philosophy—i.e., deficit reduction and fiscal responsibility—you must have enough *courage* to stand up for these principles, even if it means speaking up against the President.

As the years pass and the smoke clears from every political era, what will historians look at? They will scrutinize the character of the people involved on all sides of the political spectrum. They will look to see which ones had the courage to stand by their principles, even if this meant upsetting the President, facing the wrath of their party, betraying the people who voted for them, and risked not getting re-elected. History—which may happen within the next decade—will expose who failed these tests and, rest assured, the public and the rising generations will not be kind or forgiving. If you are ever in doubt, just look at what happened to President Nixon subsequent to Watergate and his resignation from the Presidency. Those who stood beside Nixon went down to the bottom of the ocean with his sinking ship.

While I view all of the Principles in this book as being essential, courage is a central aspect to all of them. Why? Because you cannot possibly accomplish the other nine Principles without having a backbone.

I entreat every politician—Democrat and Republican—to look at themselves in the mirror every day and say these words: "I will have the courage today to do the right thing." Having the guts to stick to one's principles is the essence of this work.

Politicians, please take heed: I know full well that they are only characters portrayed by actors, but I strongly encourage you to study and follow the examples of the following screen heroes: Mr. Smith, General Savage, Juror #8, Aron Ralston, and Captain Miller.

Of course, let's not overlook the bravery of these real-life heroines as well: Erin Brockovich (the title character of the film bearing this name, starring Julia Roberts); Maya (played by Jessica Chastain in *Zero Dark Twenty*); and Billie

Jean King (portrayed by Emma Stone in *Battle of the Sexes*).

Before we march on to our *integrity*, our next leadership principle, I will leave you with the following profound words uttered by British Prime Minister Margaret Thatcher: "Any leader has to have a certain amount of steel in them, so I am not that put out being called the Iron Lady."

PRINCIPLE #5: *Integrity*

The supreme quality for leadership is
unquestionably integrity. Without it, no real
success is possible, no matter whether it is
on a section gang, a football field,
in an army, or in an office.

—*Dwight D. Eisenhower, 34th President of the United States*

You have probably noticed that each Principle in this book is a building block on the previous one. With that in mind, you can see how *truth-seeking* and *courage* directly lead up to *integrity*. While there are certainly important aspects of *truth-seeking* and *courage* embedded in the concept of *integrity*, it is also much more than just those two things.

In my view, having integrity means not only being honest and having enough backbone to stand up for the truth, it also requires strong moral fiber and intuitively knowing how to distinguish what is right from what is wrong *at all times*. Those last three words are in italics with good reason, as you will soon see.

I'm always stunned when I come into contact with people who seem ethical out of piousness in their private lives—yet fail to demonstrate these same attributes in business. It's commendable that people teach values to their children. I applaud those who treat their relatives, friends, neighbors, and strangers with kindness, respect, and gratitude. It is admirable when that same person finds a wallet filled with cash and credit cards and then searches high and low to return it safely into the owner's hands.

Unfortunately, some of these same people have no

qualms when it comes to checking their integrity as they spin through the revolving glass doors of their office buildings. Each and every day of the year—no matter how many major scandals are exposed—someone is finding a way to take advantage of a business partner, investor, customer, supplier, colleague, or employee. On the flip side, employees also have been known to sometimes get their hands caught in the cookie jar, stealing from the business till. I've witnessed too many instances of employees entrusted with corporate credit cards who end up inappropriately buying things for their own personal benefit.

A person cannot have two faces or two personas: one upright at home, the other deceitful at work. I'm not being preachy here; in fact, I'm speaking from an entirely practical perspective; eventually, the good and bad sides always bleed together and cause disgrace from one to the other. There are always repercussions, and someone gets hurt—usually the individual and families of those who caused the offense.

In the last chapter, I delved into quite a few films that exemplify courage. I'll only bring up one in this chapter, as it magnifies the subject of cause and effect so well. At first it may seem like an off-the-wall example, but please bear with me.

You remember the classic 1960 Alfred Hitchcock thriller, *Psycho*? Yes, that's the one in which Anthony Perkins plays Norman Bates, a psychotic killer with dual personalities who stalks guests at his motel (the Bates Motel). The entire first act of the plot has nothing whatsoever to do with stabbing and mindless victimization. Janet Leigh, as secretary Marion Crane, gives in to temptation and steals $40,000 in cash at work in order to have enough money to run off with her lover (played by John Gavin). We all know what happens next: She drives off in a rainstorm and ends up stopping for the night at the Bates Motel, where she is butchered in the shower by Norman Bates (dressed as his deceased mother).

Why did I recount this gruesome story? And what on earth does this have to do with politics? Answers: If Marion Crane had resisted temptation and not stolen that money, there wouldn't have been a movie at all! She would have continued her life and survived to meet her lover on another day.

Fear not: I am in no way suggesting that Marion "deserved what she got." Nor am I preaching to you about morality. I am merely stating *cause and effect* as related to integrity. There is always some price to be paid for a misdeed. In the case of Marion Crane, her moral failure in business (stealing from her place of work) literally bled into her personal life.

INTEGRITY REQUIRES COMMITMENT AND STRENGTH

Having integrity in all aspects of one's life requires an enormous amount of commitment and fortitude. This is especially important for politicians. How many times have we seen a politician who seems to be honest on the surface but suddenly gets revealed as being corrupt? All too many, I'm afraid, and the problem is that the skeletons hidden in the back of the closet *always* get discovered. Usually these missteps ruin a politician's career, although President Donald Trump seems to be an outlier in this regard, as he was elected to office even after his offensive Access Hollywood tape was released to the public, his relationship with a porn star was exposed, and his innumerable shady business deals were reported. (They may actually have *helped* him garner support...)

For most politicians, however, scandals are a bad thing, whether they occurred before, during, or after the time frames when they held office. All you need to do is look at Bill Clinton (impeached as President), Al Franken (stepped down as Senator of Minnesota), and Gary Hart (removed himself from being a presidential candidate)—all of whom had various inappropriate incidents with women that were exposed and wrecked their reputations.

One wonders: What could these men have possibly been thinking? Didn't they realize that eventually the media would find out and have a field day reporting on their misconduct? Why enter public office in the first place if you have so much to hide?

The issue is less about morality and illegal dealings than about things such as *decency* and *trust,* which reveal how much integrity these individuals actually have. How can we respect a President and follow his leadership when we hear about his dilly-dallying with an intern in the oval office? Once we give someone the front door keys to the White House, we have an expectation that some level of decorum will be followed. If it's not, we lose respect for the President and don't trust his or her judgment on more important matters that impact hundreds of millions of people. Worse, the President should not be a person who is subject to ridicule on the world's stage; foreign powers will not take him or her seriously, whether it comes to peace talks or trade agreements with allies.

WHAT ITEMS ARE INTEGRAL TO INTEGRITY?

We are all human beings, of course, and human beings make plenty of mistakes—some are intentional, some are not. They may not be at the same level as Marion Crane in *Psycho*, but we are all capable of caving into greed, lust, and other deadly sins at one time or another. Hopefully, we learn from these lessons, make amends, and chart a new course thereafter. It is ironic that poor Marion Crane realizes the error of her ways and gives every indication that she plans to turn back and return the money the following morning; unfortunately, by the time she comes to her senses, it's too late for her to save herself.

In real life, there is only one way to bring yourself back up after a lapse: You must prove your worth by being transparent about misdeeds and displaying genuine remorse. This means hunkering down and living the straight and arrow for the rest of your days while in private and in public. One who has transgressed must work harder than ever to earn back trust and prove that integrity is part of his or her DNA.

After having fibbed to Congress and the American people, Bill Clinton finally admitted to wrongdoing. He begged forgiveness. Did this win everyone over? Probably not. But at least he had enough self-awareness and perception to realize he could not move a step forward without eating a mouthful of crow for his behavior.

President Donald Trump, on the other hand, is one in a billion: He is a narcissist who is wholeheartedly convinced that everything he does is *perfect*. Well, I have news for him: One who does not admit to mistakes, fails to show compassion and empathy, and never apologizes will never have integrity to any degree. It's an impossibility. The simple fact is that his supporters give him a free pass for everything he does, while those who are repelled by him think he is hopeless and has zero interest or capability of ever making things right—especially among those he's wronged in business and politics (who are plentiful in terms of slander, sexual misconduct, and financial dealings). While I believe every individual is responsible for his or her actions, I can at least understand why he doesn't bother making any attempts to apologize for his wrongdoing and misstatements, or give at least a passing interest in being honest: *His legions of supporters love him exactly the way he is.* To me, offering up such blind, misguided faith to a corrupt leader is like handing a loaded machine gun to a toddler. The American people deserve so much better than this!

Here are eight items I view as being integral to having integrity:

1. Demonstrating strong ethical behaviors at work each and every day.

2. Displaying strong ethical behaviors in private life each and every day.

3. Admitting to mistakes when they occur.

4. Offering sincere apologies to those who have been impacted by mistakes—both at work and at home.

5. Making amends every day after an apology has been made and proving integrity exists with each and every act and decision.

6. Expecting a high level of integrity from others and holding them accountable—especially those in political office.

7. Hiring and/or surrounding yourself with people who have a high level of integrity—even if they might disagree with you and push back on occasion.

8. Voting for politicians who value integrity.

As this book is being written, America and the entire world are being ravaged by the impact of the COVID-19 epidemic. It is taking a massive toll on human life and global economies. While Americans struggle to cope with and make sense of the spreading illness, self-quarantine, shuttered businesses, unemployment, and availability of resources (i.e., lack of protective masks, testing, hospital beds, respirators, medical teams, etc.), we look to political and medical leadership to guide us safely through these troubled times.

I will not turn this epidemic into a political issue, *however*…another integral aspect for political integrity is to be able to do the right thing *especially* when we are enduring scary episodes such as these. We are all being tested at this time. We have no need for greedy leaders who use their political posts and insider information in order to financially benefit while others lose their entire retirement savings. Politicians on both sides of the aisle, such as Senators Richard Burr, Kelly Loeffler, Jim Inhofe, and Dianne Feinstein, allegedly dumped massive amounts of stock in advance of looming Coronavirus announcements that would likely tank the markets (and ultimately did). All of these politicians had varying degrees of insider knowledge of what was about to occur prior to the public. They are being accused of having saved or made millions by their not-so-random stock decisions. Whether these politicians will be held accountable for insider trading tactics or not, there is a general consensus that this *smells bad and looks really bad*.

Our politicians have access to all kinds of confidential information and cannot allow themselves to profit from it. What did I write earlier in this book? *Government officials are elected by the people and work for the people.* We should not admire and applaud their savvy in using their political connections to fatten their own wallets and purses. They should be working for the American people and must resist temptation at all times: that is *true integrity*.

THE LAW OF ATTRACTION

The mark of people with high integrity is that it becomes second nature for them to always perform the highest quality of work in everything they do. Such exceptional performance is not rewarded by fame, titles, power, or money, but by team accomplishment and tangible results. People look up to those who have integrity. They seek to emulate them. While I believe that corrupt people tend to attract other miscreants and/or *yes* men and women, I also think the opposite is true: Integrity is contagious and can spread throughout an organization as well, including our government—as long as we are vigilant about holding our politicians accountable.

According to the Universal Law of Attraction, you inevitably attract the people and circumstances that are in harmony with your dominant thoughts and values. This means that everyone within your circle is there because of *who you are* and *how you behave*. Your integrity is manifested in your willingness to adhere to the values that are most important to you. It's easy to make promises but often extremely difficult to keep them. But every time you keep a promise that you've made, it is recognized by others as an act of integrity which, in turn, strengthens your character and how you are perceived.

PROMISES, PROMISES

Campaign promises are no exception when it comes to requiring integrity: Once a politician is elected and takes the oath of office, it is up to him or her to work toward fulfilling those obligations. You know you are in trouble right away when that leader either changes his or her mind or drops a campaign promise because it was impossible to fulfill from the beginning. In either circumstance, a politician's campaign promise is all about *integrity*. While on the campaign trail, is the politician saying he or she will do whatever it takes to get elected—even if it means making up false or unrealistic promises?

There is one notable case in history which proves that saying "whatever it takes to win" will not fly with the American people in the long run. Voters remember campaign promises and hold politicians to them. Such was the case when, during the 1988 Republican National Convention, Presidential candidate George H.W. Bush famously uttered a phrase for his campaign that bolstered himself and the Republican party: "Read my lips: No new taxes." The campaign promise became a household catchphrase that worked beyond anyone's wildest dreams: Bush ultimately became the 41st President of the United States.

Unfortunately for President Bush, the phrase worked so well it became inseparably linked with him. When the Democratic-led Senate and House proposed tax increases to battle America's deficit, the President attempted to negotiate and compromise—but failed miserably and taxes went in the exact opposite direction and were raised. The famous moniker *Read my lips: No new taxes* went from being a blessing to a downright curse for President Bush. His own words were used against him and he became a laughingstock. Members of his own party (such as Pat Buchanan) criticized him for the frittered promise. 1992 Democratic Presidential challenger Bill Clinton flayed him alive for it. This became one of the main reasons Bush did not win his re-election bid. Voters feel angry and betrayed when campaign promises are not met—especially when it's been publicly delivered with such fierce determination, as was the case with President Bush.

History is riddled with such examples from American leaders in both parties. Some politicians were well-meaning at first, but then backed off the campaign promise as reality set in or when they were forced to cave to political pressure. Here are some notable cases:

- President Woodrow Wilson became re-elected based on his promise to keep America out of a war. Less than one year later, the United States entered World War I.

- In 1964, President Lyndon B. Johnson made it clear he did not wish to send American troops to Vietnam. Over the next few years, Johnson ordered 125,000 U.S. soldiers to Vietnam.

- In 1968, President Richard Nixon claimed he had a "secret plan" to end the Vietnam War. This turned out to be an outright lie, as troops were not withdrawn from Vietnam until five years later, in 1973.

- Bill Clinton ran his political campaign based on health care reform. He could not gain support for his "Hillarycare" concept," and it took several years to manifest under President Barack Obama as Obamacare.

There is no way around the fact that political rhetoric is required for political candidates. They have to make bold promises in order to get attention, gain support, and win the election. Phraseology and circumstance are crucial aspects, however. Empty and/or exaggerated promises just to obtain votes reveal a lack of integrity, especially if the candidate doesn't have a clue as to whether the promise is possible to achieve.

In 2016, when Donald Trump promised to build a wall and "Mexico will pay for it," many of his followers actually believed him. On the positive side for his supporters, Trump never let go of his promise once he entered office; he had every intent on fulfilling his end of the bargain. The problem? There was no way in a million years he would ever be able to convince Mexico to pay for his prized border wall. Nor could he convince Congress to cough up enough money in the budget to build it. With nowhere else to go, he declared a dubious "national emergency" about the state of illegal immigration across the Mexican border to be able to tap into funding.

Construction of the border wall commenced, but several billion came from American counter-drug operations, while even more was redirected from military construction accounts. Who is paying for America's border wall? *America*—to the tune of $7.2 billion!

The upshot is that, although Trump is fulfilling a campaign promise to build a Mexican border wall, he deflated the effort by making it seem as if Mexico would pay for it through increased tariffs, which is clearly not the case. The means to achieve the ends *do matter*, and the President's exaggerations once again speak to an utter lack of integrity.

Ultimately, the buck stops with the politician. Realistic, achievable campaign promises may sound boring, won't make headlines, and may not help the politician get ahead of the pack, but they do speak to a politician who has credibility, can get things done, and has integrity. We must be skeptical of false promises that we know are mere pipe dreams.

In the next Principle, we will cover subjects that are the essence of what America has been all about since its founding: *tolerance and equality*. Unfortunately, all too often human bias, ignorance, and prejudice have risen up and caused America to go several steps backwards instead of making forward progress in these important areas.

PRINCIPLE #6: *Tolerance and Equality*

It is never too late to give up your prejudices.

—Henry David Thoreau, 19th century essayist and philosopher

In the wake of a major health epidemic in San Francisco, a young Asian woman is spit on by a man who blames her race for the spread of the disease.

In Brooklyn, New York, a woman is charged with committing three assaults in one day against different Hassidic Jewish women.

At Eastern Illinois University in Charleston, IL, bags filled with rocks and white power propaganda ("White Power, Get Some!") are discovered all over campus.

You might think the above instances happened in the 1960s or perhaps even earlier, but all of these hate crimes—and hundreds more—occurred in the United States in the first quarter of 2020. Every time I think we have made at least some kind of progress in our country against prejudice, hate, violence, discrimination, and inequality, a news flash pops up indicating that we have been heading in the exact opposite direction.

Dealing with prejudice and inequality should not have to be a "next big thing in politics" or in any other part of society. Unfortunately, the situation has become so rampant and dire in America that it must not only be addressed, it must be swatted away and squashed forever.

The sobering statistics are as follows:

- Between 2015-2017, the number of reported hate crimes increased 17% after years of decline.

- From 2017 to 2018, the number of hate crimes remained relatively flat at around 7,100, but the number of crimes targeting religion and race were both up.

- In 2015 and 2016, the percentage of anti-Semitic incidents were 51%-54% of the total number; during the years 2017 and 2018, this number shot up to 59%-60%.

What is happening here? It's no secret that prejudice and inequality have existed below and above the surface before and after our country was founded, and these circumstances continue through present day. Slavery may no longer exist, but vestiges of racial bias and inequality still remain in our society. According to the Pew Center, four out of ten Americans believe that black people do not have the same equal rights and opportunities as white people. Common perceptions are that black people have far less potential to garner wealth and be hired for top executive positions in our country today. They are also a much greater target for racial profiling by police.

These are far from the only areas where discrimination exists. As of March 2020, women earn nineteen cents on the dollar less than men. This is a two-cent improvement above 2019, but still far from acceptable.

I do not mean to give any pretense that I am a liberal, a so-called socialist, or any other moniker along those lines. I am merely stating the facts and imploring us to do much better across the board, especially in politics. Every American has the right to equal opportunity and should not have any fear whatsoever of discrimination. In my view, life and liberty in our country means that *all lives matter* and *all lives are equal.* I have zero tolerance for any statements and actions to the contrary.

WHAT IS HAPPENING IN THE LAND OF THE FREE?

Although I believe that prejudice has always resided in the minds of many people to varying degrees, circumstances have arisen these past few years that have enabled people to feel that it's okay to publicly express their biased views, citing the right of free speech.

Our freedom comes with great responsibility, however; we must respect the rights and liberties of others at all times. As British philosopher John Stuart Mill wrote in *On Liberty*:

> *The only freedom which deserves the name is that of pursuing our own good in our own way, so long as we do not attempt to deprive others of theirs, or impede their efforts to obtain it. Each is the proper guardian of his own health, whether bodily, or mental or spiritual. Mankind are greater gainers by suffering each other to live as seems good to themselves, than by compelling each to live as seems good to the rest.*

In other words, we are entitled to enjoy our own individual freedoms to the fullest extent, as long as we don't stop others from attempting to express their own such rights and liberties. As soon as you cross that line and hinder someone else's rights, you have transgressed.

There is an important lesson to be learned from the

Neo-Nazi rally (dubbed "Unite the Right") that took place in Charlottesville, VA, on August 12, 2017. Harkening back to the Nazi march that took place in Skokie, IL, on April 19, 1978—uncoincidentally, the home of some 7,000 Holocaust survivors—the Charlottesville incident involved white nationalists raising lit tiki torches and chanting "blood and soil" (a phrase associated with Nazi Germany). A state of emergency was announced when pro-testers appeared to counter the marchers. Violence broke out. The worst came in the form of a white nationalist named James Alex Fields, who plowed his car into a crowd of counter-protesters. Thirty-two-year old Heather Heyer was murdered, and nineteen others were injured.

This tragedy stands as one of the greatest blemishes to ever take place on American soil. *Americans vs. Americans.* Any way we look at it, this is ghastly and abhorrent. Why did such a terrible thing occur? I'll tell you: It happened because one side chose hatred over civility.

And how did our 45th President react? From his golf club in New Jersey, President Donald Trump made the follow-ing announcement: "We condemn in the strongest possible terms this egregious display of hatred, bigotry, and violence on many sides—on many sides."

Huh? How *many sides* were there? Was he proclaiming that Heather Heyer, the victim, deserved to be struck dead by a car? Were there people on more than "one side" driv-ing cars into crowds?

Of course, there weren't. Only *one side was at fault*: American white nationalists. President Trump did what he always does: He placed blame all around, so he would not upset white nationalists—a group of people who proudly support him. President Trump did not wish to offend any-one, which might alienate his base, hurt his approval rat-ing, and cause him to lose voters in the future.

This was reprehensible, to say the least. Instead of building bridges, comforting those who were hurt, and fully condemning only those who deserved it, the President was winking at the white nationalists as if to say, "I've got your back." As a result, the white nationalists felt validated, empowered, and ultimately strengthened by the President's reactions. To be sure, there hasn't been a President in modern history who acted with such disregard for victims since...well, *ever*.

We have already established in previous Principles that the President of the United States must represent *all* citizens and do so with *integrity*—not just the people who voted for him or her. The vast majority of Americans are good people who believe in equal rights, religious freedom, and liberty for all, whereas white nationalists do not. It is an abomination that the President, of all people, pandered to such a minority of racists. His statement caused even greater rifts throughout our nation, as I will now explain....

DOES POLITICAL RHETORIC REALLY INCITE RACISM?

A large number of people who support President Trump do not believe that he is racist or deny that his words encourage racism. (Some may indeed be racists themselves, whether they realize it or not—but that isn't for me to decide.) They assert that it's "just Trump being Trump" and he is entitled to say and do whatever he wants. They think it's simply business as usual for him to spout controversial things and put his foot in his mouth without paying any consequences.

This begs the questions: *Do words really matter? Does President Trump's statement about bad behavior on "both sides" in the Charlottesville incident really have impact—or do his blind followers simply dismiss this as "just Trump being Trump"?*

The answers are *Yes*: The evidence has shown that political rhetoric does incite racism, anti-Semitism, and hate crimes in general. Subsequent to Charlottesville, David Duke—the longtime Ku Klux Klan leader—felt validated in saying, "We are determined to take our country back…. We are going to fulfill the promises of Donald Trump. That's what we believed in. That's why we voted for Donald Trump, because he said he's going to take our country back."

It's scary times when the President of the United States can inspire a KKK leader to such magnitude. Yet nary a GOP Senator did a blessing thing to help curb the damage and make Americans feel safer from these potential internal threats against fellow Americans.

At Trump's political rallies from 2015 to present, he has made some pretty xenophobic, racist, and sexist remarks. When he had political disputes with Senators Alexandria Ocasio Cortez, Rashida Tlaib, Ayanna Pressley, and Ilhan Omar, Trump lambasted them at his political rallies and used the offensive phrase "send them back."

Where should they be sent, exactly? All four of these women are American citizens! Either he meant returning them to their crime-infested neighborhoods or, more likely, to their places of origin based on their ethnicity. A political difference is one thing, but a President saying "send them back" to four American citizens of color who happen to disagree with him is truly a racist on an entirely different level.

The data is pretty clear. There is an obvious correlation between Trump's rhetoric and the increase in hate crimes in the United States. Statistically, the rise in number of hate crimes was disproportionately higher in locations where

President Trump won a large percentage of votes in the 2016 Presidential election. The increase that occurred after his Presidential victory was only matched by the number of hate crimes against Muslims post-9/11. Areas that hosted a Trump rally had *double* the likelihood of hate crimes taking place.

What did the President do about all of this violence that broke out in the wake of his off-the-cuff speeches? *Absolutely nothing.*

IMMIGRATION CONFLATION

I admit that immigration is a loaded topic. Let me be more specific: *Illegal* immigration is a charged subject. I have no objection whatsoever to individuals who arrive in America through the proper legal channels. There is nothing to substantiate the claim that legal immigrants contribute anything negative to American society. I would argue that it's quite the opposite and they enrich American culture.

On the other hand, *illegal* immigration has been a major issue in America for longer than anyone can remember, and there are compelling arguments from all points of view, although precious few sensible solutions have been offered by either political side.

I empathize with people who flee to America to escape persecution in their home countries. I understand why they would risk the lives of their children and themselves to cross dangerous borders to reach freedom's shores and obtain a brighter future.

Public safety is indeed an issue here in America, and we must be vigilant about protecting ourselves. Of course, background checks are crucial to ensuring the individuals entering our country are not a threat to our security. There must also be a clear pathway to achieving citizenship for individuals without criminal records. Our country has been built upon the myriad accomplishments of immigrants from all around the globe.

That said, as I've previously stated, illegal immigration should be treated as a major concern. America does not need or want additional threats in the form of terrorism or crimes associated with drug and/or human trafficking. Our nation must also figure out how to first handle its own poverty, homelessness, medical care, and unemployment before we can support immigrant families.

To battle illegal immigration, do we need a border wall around Mexico to keep out "bad *hombres*" (another offensive racial slur from our President)? Should we be afraid that migrant workers might steal job opportunities away from hard-working Americans? Is it necessary to separate immigrant children from their families and lock them in cages? Must we ban people of certain religions and ethnic backgrounds, implying that they are all evil?

Let me assure you that I wholeheartedly believe in and support strong borders. I also think we must take necessary precautions to protect Americans from terrorism. The lessons of 9/11 are emblazoned in all of our collective memories. When deciding upon a political stance and course of action, it all becomes a matter of finding the right balance among these considerations:

- What did the Founding Fathers put in writing?

- What are the guiding precepts that have built and sustained our nation?

- How do we represent ourselves on the world's stage as a symbolic guiding humanitarian force?

- What is the genuine threat of crime entering our nation across our borders and into our ports and airports?

- What is the reality of American jobs being threatened by an influx of immigrants?

- What is the cost of assimilating immigrants into our country and can we afford it?

- How does the human suffering of the individuals wishing to enter our country balance against our job and economic concerns?

- How can we enforce a humane policy to deter illegal and potentially threatening immigration to our country while at the same time offering safe refuge for people whose lives and rights are under attack every day?

- How do we create an affordable solution for undocumented immigrants whose families have been in this country for years without draining valuable American resources and potentially bankrolling a few potential terrorists and criminals?

I saved the most important question for last: *How do we create an effective policy that does not discriminate against any singular ethic group, race, religion, nationality, sexual orientation, or class?*

The one thing we are not: Nazi Germany in the 1940s. We are a country made up of immigrants who have built and sustained our country over the years, including: Albert Einstein (Germany), Arnold Schwarzenegger (Austria),

Enrico Fermi (Mexico), Madeleine Albright (Prague), Sofia Vergara (Colombia), Bob Marley (Jamaica), Elon Musk (South Africa), Penelope Cruz (Spain), Levi Strauss (Germany), Audrey Hepburn (Belgium), Arianna Huffington (Greece), Joseph Pulitzer (Hungary), Jackie Chan (China), Ayn Rand (Russia), Carlos Santana (Mexico), Andrew Carnegie (Scotland), Nikola Tesla (Croatia), etc. Did any of these individuals turn out to be "bad *hombres*"?

We are not a "white" or singularly "Christian" nation. We are a country that bleeds red, white, and blue, and we must be accepting of people of all persuasions and beliefs who honor and respect our laws. Once you are proclaimed an "American Citizen"—whether from birth or the official naturalization process—you are one for life. It doesn't matter which country you originated from.

This means that all of the bluster you have been hearing the past several years about threats from so-called "rapists and bad *hombres*" coming in from Mexico is a bunch of bull. Yes, we need to protect our borders against the drug cartels and such, but name-calling and building a symbolic wall separating us from Mexico is certainly not the answer. The American people have been misled by right wing leadership that suffers from a bad case of xenophobia.

These are the statistics pre-initiation of President Trump's border wall that "Mexico was going to pay for":

- Illegal immigration from Mexico declined by two million people between 2007 and 2017.

- Less than half (38%) of all border arrests were related to illegal immigration.

- There is no statistical evidence one way or the other indicating that illegal immigrants cause more crime in the United States than natural-born citizens.

- In areas surrounding the Mexican border, the United States has not witnessed any kind of tangible relationship between illegal immigration and crime.

So why did President Trump claim a National State of Emergency in order to get his executive order for a border wall funded? Further, why did he also enact a Muslim ban preventing people from Iran, Libya, Somalia, Syria, and Yemen from entering the United States when the statistics reveal that an American citizen is *253 times more likely* to be murdered by someone other than a terrorist from these countries?

The answer is simple: President Trump has been playing to racial and religious intolerance as a way to create the perception of a common enemy targeting "true Americans." Fear, ignorance, and prejudice can serve as powerful weapons to claim power. Unfortunately, as stated earlier, the weaponization of falsehoods leads to an increase in hate crimes and divides the nation even further. We cannot live in irrational fear of our neighbors because they look, speak, pray, or dress differently than we do. Indeed, the greatest threats to our nation are ignorance and believing the lies and misstatements of our President.

A POSITIVE LIGHT FROM THE DARKNESS

That said, not everything the President has done has been hurtful to our minorities. Buried within the Tax Cuts and Jobs Act of 2017 (known as the TCJA), President Trump approved legislation Subchapter Z, which encourages investing in areas that can achieve tax savings and contribute to the greater good. My book, *Opportunity Investing: How to Revitalize Urban and Rural Communities With Opportunity Funds,* lays out how investing in Qualified Opportunity Zones (QOZs) with Qualified Opportunity Zones (QOZs) can help some 8,800 approved distressed areas all over our nation. Not only does this legislation provide the means to boost less fortunate communities, it is unbiased in its messaging about race, creed, religion, or country of origin. This is the first time the government has approved an initiative that is beneficial to the financial community *and* also to struggling communities without providing handouts; it's a win-win for everyone.

I bring this up not as a plug for my book (which will be discussed further in Principle #9), but rather, to demonstrate that we don't have to use offensive, discriminatory language while attempting to manage illegal immigration, stop terrorism, or resolve any other issue in our country. We should not be pointing fingers at a specific race or religious group to blame them for the ills of our society; that is not the American way. We need humane solutions that treat people with dignity and respect and do not separate families or cage helpless children. We must stop labeling pandemics by country names (i.e., "Chinese Virus" for COVID-19), which leads to unnecessary victimization of true-blue, hard-working Americans who happen to be Asian Americans.

Politicians, please take serious heed: Civility is the long-term answer to unifying our country and "making it great again"—not bigotry, sexism, anti-Semitism, or any other form of prejudice. All we need to do is celebrate diversity and practice the art of *inclusion*, not exclusion.

This is the perfect segue to our very next principle, which is spelled out magnificently in the song by legendary singer Aretha Franklin: R-E-S-P-E-C-T.

PRINCIPLE #7: *Respect*

People who hold certain institutional
positions should have your respect until
they lose it. But the rest of us
mortals have to earn it.

—John McCain, former United States Senator

The date: October 10, 2008.
The place: Lakeville High School, Lakeville, MN.
The subject: John McCain's town hall meeting.

*[A white-haired Minnesota woman wearing a McCain/
Palin tee-shirt takes the microphone to directly address
Republican Presidential nominee, John McCain, who
stands before her.]*

Minnesota Woman: *I gotta' ask you a question. I can't
trust Obama. I have read about him, and he's not, um,
he's an Arab.*

Senator McCain *(emphatically shaking his head)*:
*No…no, ma'm. He's a decent family man, citizen that I
just happen to have disagreements with on fundamental
issues, and that's what this campaign is all about. He's
not [an Arab].*

Why, you may ask, is the above scene from 2008
worth bringing up to start this Principle? Because
it represents all of the wonderful potential residing inside,
yet buried deep within, American politics: goodness, honesty, courage and, most of all, *respect*. Many candidates on

both sides of the aisle would have either agreed with a citizen trashing a political adversary or have allowed it to pass without comment.

What did Senator John McCain do by deflating the woman's assertion? I can tell you what he *did not* do: utter a single negative word against his opponent, instead choosing to take the controversial path of *defending* Obama and his values. (He also could have taken the opportunity that there is nothing wrong with being an Arab, but his reaction on the spur of the moment was genuine and spontaneous; he clearly did not wish to give the woman's comments too much attention.)

It's hard to believe how far we have gone down the wrong path in the past dozen plus years since McCain spoke up at that town hall. Attacks against an individual's political views are one thing, but personal insults are another. Over the past few years, President Trump—yes, we must head down this road again—has described his political rivals in the following manner on Twitter and/or in his campaign speeches and interviews:

- **Former Vice-President Joe Biden:** sleepycreepy Joe; another low-IQ individual; quid pro Joe

- **Senator Bernie Sanders:** crazy Bernie

- **Democratic Presidential Candidate Hillary Clinton**: crooked Hillary; nasty woman

- **Senator Elizabeth Warren:** Pocahontas; fake Pocahontas; goofy Elizabeth Warren; the Indian

- **Congressman Beta O'Rourke:** a flake; stone-cold phony

- **Senator Amy Klobuchar:** snowman(woman)

- **Senator Kirsten Gillibrand:** lightweight senator

- **Senator Kamala Harris:** very nasty

- **Mayor Pete Buttigieg:** Alfred E. Neuman

- **Mayor Bill de Blasio:** worst mayor in the U.S.

- **Former Mayor Mike Bloomberg:** little Michael Bloomberg; mini Mike

- **Senator Adam Schiff:** Little Adam Schitt

- **President Barack Obama:** Cheatin' Obama

These are just a few labels he's assigned to others and, as you can see, they run the gamut of disparaging remarks about physical appearance, ethnicity, gender, and behavioral quirks. He has even mimicked physically challenged individuals through body language. Whether the insults have any truth to them does not matter one bit; they are immature and unbecoming of any elected official (or any leader, *period*). Usage of profanity is particularly offensive, inappropriate, and crude.

President Trump: Please, I beg you, *stop*.

NO RESPECT

When late stand-up comedian Rodney Dangerfield said the words "no respect," he was referring to himself in self-deprecating terms. Take this one liner, for example: "When I was a kid my parents moved around a lot, but I found them." Dangerfield was allowing himself to be the on the receiving end of his insults, which is what made them so funny.

Other comedians, such as Groucho Marx, Don Rickles, Joan Rivers and, more recently, Jeff Ross, made entire careers out of insulting and disrespecting other people. People laughed. Audiences adored them without being offended. Why did they get away with their slurs? Because they were *paid comedians,* and everyone knew full well they were only joking. If anything, they were making social commentary by satirizing pretentiousness, bigotry, sexism, and hypocritical behavior.

As of this writing, President Trump is still President of the United States of America. He was *not* elected by the American people to serve as a standup insult comic. He may have been a TV reality show host at one time (*The Apprentice*) who had a certain persona (i.e., when he would say "you're fired" with relish to contestants)—but that was mere entertainment.

While humor is an important aspect of Principle #2 (Leadership), being Commander-in-Chief of the world's greatest country is very serious business. Knowing when to apply humor and hold back is crucial, and it's never a good thing for one American citizen to personally insult another. We could get into the weeds spouting the litany of catch-phrases and nicknames others have used against President Trump but, as former First Lady Michelle Obama famously said, "When they go low, we go high."

CALL BULL ON THE SCHOOL BULLY

President Trump would actually garner much greater respect—and potentially a wider base—if he were to simply stick to his scripts and avoid lashing out at his perceived adversaries. Who cares if a politician is below average height? What possible implication does this have on the issues surrounding our country? What right does Donald Trump have to judge others?

None—except that it speaks to the fact that he is the most disrespectful President our country has ever had. He is acting the part of the school bully while ruling the playground of the most powerful office in the world. As cited in Principle #6, words can—and do—have serious impact.

On the wall of virtually every elementary school, middle school, and high school class in our country, you can find a poster featuring images of our forty-five Presidents. Students passing by it do one of three things: absorb it for learning purposes; ignore it; or regard these men with such respect they want to someday hold that prestigious office. The President is a person to be admired and respected, whose chief characteristics are held in high enough esteem to deserve emulation.

Various reports have documented that President's Trump's inflammatory remarks—against politicians, celebrities, and pretty much anyone who doesn't lavish praise on him—have filtered down and caused reverberations throughout our school hallways. In February 2020, *The Washington Post* reported that schools have witnessed a dramatic increase in school bullying. From 2016-2019, at least 300 specific harassment incidents were reported in schools that had been influenced in some tangible fashion by President Trump. Among those, 75% included language that correlates between President Trump's verbiage against Muslims, black people, and Hispanics with those of student against student.

At a high school football game in Kennewick, WA, chants broke out against Hispanic schoolmates along the lines of: "Make America Great Again!" and "Build the Wall!" Elsewhere in our nation, at a high school in Shakopee, MN, boys clad in Donald Trump shirts surrounded a black girl and taunted her by singing "The Star-Spangled Banner" with an altered last line: "…and the home of the slaves" instead of "home of the brave."

Respect goes upwards, downwards, and sideways. Our children hear, see, feel, and repeat everything that adults say, especially those who have positions of authority and large Twitter feeds (as our President does). Instead of serving as a role model for our youth, our President is teaching and spreading hate to a whole new generation of children.

All of this is quite ironic, especially considering the fact that First Lady Melania Trump initiated a "Be Best" campaign in 2018 that includes anti-bullying measures. It's unclear what, if anything, Be Best has actually accomplished on this front. One thing is for sure: It would be far more successful if the First Lady could have some measure of positive influence on her own husband's behavior.

POURING GASOLINE ON THE FIRE

Mind you, respect is not a one-way street. Several Democrats have also failed the respect test, allowing themselves to be drawn into the schoolyard brawl. In June 2018, California Congresswoman Maxine Waters said the following at a Los Angeles rally: "If you see anybody from that Cabinet in a restaurant, in a department store, at a gasoline station, you get out and you create a crowd and you push back on them and you tell them they're not welcome anymore, anywhere."

This statement was made after two Trump administration officials—Homeland Security Secretary Kirstjen Nielsen and White House Press Secretary Sarah Huckabee Sanders—were each harassed while dining at different public restaurants. The owners of Red Hen restaurant in Lexington, VA went as far as refusing Ms. Huckabee service because of her job title and support of the President (especially his immigration policy).

The cliché "two wrongs don't make a right" seems appropriate here. If Ms. Waters has a point to make about the President's policies, she has hundreds of ways to express it that are far more civil and respectful than encouraging the public humiliation of elected government officials and the people selected by them.

Throughout this Principle, I have referenced comedians who fired off insults against others or themselves, all within the boundaries of good humor. On May 30, 2017, comedienne Kathy Griffin stepped far outside those boundaries by posting a photograph on her Twitter feed of herself holding a severed, bloodied Trump head. There is such a thing as crossing the line—and then there is Ms. Griffin's act, which was the equivalent of cartoon character Wile E. Coyote falling off a cliff.

Lord only knows what the comedienne had been thinking, but any objective, rationale mind would have regarded her post as gravely offensive and disrespectful. It's one thing to imagine terrible things about a leader and possibly even commiserate with friends and family about it; it's a whole other to publicly express the desire to inflict bodily harm upon another person (especially the President).

Predictably, the backlash against Ms. Griffin was swift and severe. Liberal, Democrat, and Republican alike condemned it. Her career plummeted, as comedy club owners and television producers didn't want anything to do with her. In spite of her tearful apologies, Ms. Griffin was labeled an ISIS terrorist and placed on a "no fly list" with airlines. She even received several personal death threats from supporters of the President.

When one is bullied in grade school, the impulse is to toughen up and stand up to him or her. The thinking is that most young bullies are actually afraid, jealous, and/or insecure and will back down when personally confronted.

This is not the case when it comes to responding to

political bullying and name-calling from the President. Whether he has insulted or offended you by his comments and/or Tweets, utilizing the same tactics back at him is never the best course of action. It's perfectly fine to disagree with the President when it comes to the issues and on policy—last time I checked we were still a Democracy—but engaging in the game of insults with him or anyone else is stooping to that same level and only stokes the flames of Twitter fires. When the smoke clears from the Trump Presidency, we must be certain our slates—as well as our collective conscience—are 100% clean, or we will never have complete self-respect and certainly will not regain the respect of others.

PRACTICING RESPECTFUL RULES OF ENGAGEMENT

We will delve much more into the art of *compromise* in Principle #10. For now, let's hold tight and present ways in which Republicans and Democrats alike can exemplify partisan respect while engaging each other in all matters, including when it comes to major policy disagreement.

First, let's remove President #45 from this equation for the purposes of this discussion and presume that respect begins and ends at the top. As stated, the President should serve as the role model, which is currently not the case. If we were to strip away his vindictive comments and behavior, we will have already clamped down on at least some of the need for politicians to act rudely and disrespectfully to each other. A portion of this has been a result of people defending or attacking the President's policies or Tweets. A good chunk has also been to pander to his ego and win his favor (i.e., Senator Lindsey Graham). Or, as Democrats must be willing to admit, there is a continuous spiteful undercurrent against the President in reaction to his history of vitriol. All of this nonsense is unnecessary and both sides are playing a childish game that politicians will never win—and which, ultimately, the American people will lose.

Respectful Rule #1: Admit That Respect Must Be Mutual

This first rule may seem obvious but, based on a Pew Research Center study, a lot of work still needs to be done. Most Americans (68%) feel that our elected officials must be respectful to members of the other party. The balance tips somewhat higher to Democrats (72%) than Republicans (63%).

This suggests there is room to be optimistic, right? *Respect* is clearly important to everyone.

When you probe further, however, it reveals that both Democrats and Republicans expect the other party to be more respectful to them (75%-78% range) than the reverse (47%-49% range). So, the majority expects a great deal more on the *receiver* side than on the *giver* side. This strikes me as quite selfish and automatically incites distrust. In any discourse, both sides must agree to mutually respect each other right out of the gate.

Respectful Rule #2: Acknowledge the Opposition's Point of View

Human resource business professionals often use the phrase *active listening* when it comes to best practices involving personal interaction, such as between a supervisor and her direct report. It's no different in politics. Active listening not only involves practicing good body language (such as eye contact) with the other individual and giving him or her the opportunity to speak openly, it also means verbally acknowledging the person's statement afterwards.

For example, if a Republican says something along the

lines of "My community is deeply concerned about illegal immigrants taking away their jobs," the Democratic response should not be "That's a bunch of bull and you know it. Immigrants do jobs no one else wants."

Why? Because it sends a message right away that the Democrat refuses to listen, is set in his ways, and therefore doesn't care what the Republican has to say.

Instead, the Democrat might open with something along the lines of: "I hear what you are saying. I get it. No one wants *illegal* immigrants overtaking our country, nor do we want anyone stealing jobs away from hard-working Americans."

There you have it: Respectful dialogue has been initiated. The Republican feels *acknowledged* without being antagonized and dismissed. In fact, in this scenario, the pair has immediately discovered common ground, which is a good place to start.

Respectful Rule #3: Keep Emotions in Check... Except, Maybe, for a Couple

Problems surface anytime emotional levels rise. Politicians, in particular, need to bury signs of bubbling emotions while involved in discourse. When fear and anger come into play, voices are raised, fists are clenched, and teeth are gritted. In this regard, people seem to react like dogs: They don't understand the other person's emotional response and, in turn, behave emotionally. If one side growls or barks, the other feels the need to prove he or she is the bigger dog and growl or bark back even louder.

Here's the first possible exception: *empathy*. If you demonstrate genuine empathy to the other person's situation, you will automatically turn the other person around to being receptive to your point of view. It shows that you care about the other person, even if you happen to disagree.

The second exception: *humor*. When used appropriately,

a timely joke can lighten a mood and also allow room for common ground. As in any circumstance, you have to be careful you don't inadvertently say something inappropriate that might offend the other party (or someone not in the room who might hear about it).

Sarcasm is always a bad idea when involved in political dialogue—unless it involves self-deprecation. Ronald Reagan (also singled out for his humorous touch in Principle #2) had a clever way of turning a situation around, yet still managed to come across as affable because he would feel comfortable enough to take a potshot at himself. When asked if he was in any way responsible for the Recession of the early 1980s, he remarked: "Yes, because for many years I was a Democrat."

Respectful Rule #5: Always Provide Concrete Examples

Statistics can often be manipulated, misinterpreted, and even fabricated in order to attempt to prove a point in a political disagreement. As I've repeatedly stated in this work, *the truth matters. Facts matter.* Always rely on trusted, impartial sources while making your case. In other words, anything smacking of the far left or the far right will only get an eyeroll from the opposition. If a Republican were to cite a Fox News poll to a Democrat, for example, the latter would automatically jump to the conclusion that it is biased; in fact, that individual might feel disrespected at having that particular media source thrown in his or her face.

Instead, provide concrete examples from non-partisan sources. If, for example, a Democratic politician wishes to make a case that the American policy on illegal immigration is inhumane, she might calmly present an example of a Mexican family that has been separated: The parents were sent back to Mexico, while their six-year-old daughter

(Carmen) and two-year-old brother (Juan) have been holed up in cages along the border for six months.

Would some people not care to hear or even believe this sad story? Possibly. But at least respect has been paid to the listener and that helps maintain civility all around. The Republican will at least remember the respectful treatment the next time he is in contact with that same Democrat and behave in reciprocal fashion.

Respectful Rule #6: Admit That Your Party Is Imperfect

This medicine might be hard for many people to swallow, no matter which side of the political spectrum they fall on. Politicians are sometimes too afraid to admit they are human beings capable of making mistakes because the press will cast them in a bad light, the party will deride them, or it "gives points away to the other team."

I see much better logic to a strategy that occasionally involves eating a slice of humble pie. Sometimes, when two parties are far apart in terms of ideology, it helps to take one on the chin—absorbing at least some blame—in order to bridge the gap and help the bigger picture.

For example, a Democrat might say: "Yes, I admit it. We made an error with the last piece of legislation that led to a tax increase. Neither side ended up happy with it." Or, it could be a more general type of statement along the lines of: "Let's face it. We've both made a lot of mistakes, myself included. We'd like to make amends on that front. This piece of legislation is good for Republicans *and* Democrats—and we can all benefit from the shared credit and teamwork because we are working jointly for the people."

At the end of the day, we want our government to get things done for the American people. In fact, they are being *paid* to be respectful toward each other and to search for mutually agreeable solutions. Our politicians need to demonstrate that they are working for us and not serving as blind cheerleaders for their team or as partisan squawk boxes, posturing and firing nasty missives across the aisle.

During the painfully sad moments of the televised funerals of Senator Elijah E. Cummings, President George H. W. Bush, and Senator John McCain, I felt some measure of American pride witnessing the fact that many members of both parties paid their heartfelt respects to these esteemed political servants. Conservative Senator Mark Meadows may have been on the exact opposite end of the political spectrum from Senator Cummings, yet he was quoted as saying the following in tribute: "I will miss him dearly."

Now *that* is a sign of genuine respect. Unfortunately, it begs the question: *Why can't kind statements ever seem to occur while these respected figures are still alive?*

In our next Principle, we will address a subject I know all Americans agree upon at its core: *patriotism.*

PRINCIPLE #8: *Patriotism*

True patriotism springs from a belief in
the dignity of the individual, freedom, and
equality not only for Americans but for all
people on earth, universal brotherhood,
and good will, and a constant and earnest
striving toward the principles and ideals on
which this country was founded.

—*Eleanor Roosevelt, 1st Lady of the United States*

Patriotism. What does it really mean—and how is it best
exemplified?

Is it displaying or waving an American flag on July 4th?
Is it honoring our veterans marching in a Memorial Day
parade? Is it casting a ballot for a candidate on election day?
Is it joining a protest against a policy that might be hurtful
to fellow citizens? Do you have to love baseball, hotdogs,
and apple pie in order to be considered a patriot?

You certainly do not need to be a fan of the New England
Patriots football team to be a patriot. You don't even have
to like team owner Robert Kraft to appreciate his patriotic
act in April 2020 when, at his own expense, he shipped
5,000 protective masks on his private plane to New York
to help the medical community treat COVID-19 patients.
There is an aspect of selflessness at the heart of patriotism,
as well as a feeling of pride and admiration toward those
who perform such acts.

Patriotism can mean many things and vary depending
upon the circumstances involved. Obviously, patriotism
rises when a country is defending itself against a commonly
perceived threat from a specific enemy. It can have deeply

emotional—and possibly even spiritual—overtones for many people. There is an inherent individualism to how one believes in his or her country and expresses such personal devotion. At the same time, there is an implied collective social aspect to patriotism—i.e., a belief that: *We—our countrymen and countrywomen—are all in this together.*

Now, more than ever, patriotism is essential to the restoration of our government after years of ugly internal political conflicts.

THE TRUE MEANING OF PATRIOTISM VS. NATIONALISM

It's commonly accepted that *patriotism* means "love for one's country." Many people take it a step further to state that it requires your willingness to "die for your country." Indeed, American soldiers put their lives on the line every day on behalf of our country, and there is no doubt in my mind that each and every American service person past and present has gone above and beyond qualifying for the moniker of *patriot*.

Nationalism, by contrast, is patriotism on steroids. When one takes a nationalistic stance, he or she loves the country so wholeheartedly it signals the exclusion of other countries—even, potentially, Americans who belong to certain ethnic or religious groups, as well as important global allies. I would go out on a limb to put forth the notion that, if you consider yourself a *nationalist*, you are not a true American patriot.

In my view, the problem with American nationalism is that we are a country built by immigrants and refugees from other nations. (Let's also not forget to include slaves brought here against their will in the past.) Many people arrived in America in order to escape persecution from elsewhere and to enjoy all of the freedoms our country has to offer. Nationalism in America can, therefore, be a scary thing for many people, as it has been accepted by certain racist groups to refer only to "white America" with the intent of breeding prejudice, discrimination, and hate.

The paradox we struggle with as Americans is that it's entirely possible to be a dedicated patriot and yet be far removed from nationalistic thinking. Part of our wonderful democracy is that we have the right to openly express our disagreement with government policy and actions, yet still be considered a patriot. In a Democracy, we don't blindly follow our leaders—especially if we believe they are headed down the wrong path. I believe that being an American patriot also means allowing room for other perspectives, as long as you don't betray our laws or contradict the ideals of our Founding Fathers and Mothers. This means you should never be accused of being unpatriotic if you belong to a different political party, vote for a certain candidate (unless such a person is a proven criminal or enemy of the people), or challenge the government (again, within the boundaries of what is legal and civil behavior). In fact, I would suggest that those who indiscriminately accuse people of being unpatriotic for these reasons are hindering free thought and Democracy and, therefore, are behaving in an *un*patriotic manner.

We are not judge, jury, and verdict empowered with gavels to determine "who is patriotic versus who isn't." One political party cannot assert having greater patriotism than the other. This harkens back to the aforementioned concept of patriotism as being a deeply personal and potentially religious concept. You may observe your country every single day of the year or only on national holidays, yet in both cases be a bona-fide American patriot.

On the other hand, I have firm conviction in supporting and respecting our military men and women. As a veteran myself (of the Vietnam War), I understand all too well from firsthand experience what a solider endures on the battlefield and also what it's like to return to civilian life afterwards. Removing a hat and placing your hand over your heart during "The Star-Spangled Banner" at a ball-game (as well as when it's played anywhere else) is the least we can all do to honor our soldiers who put their lives on the line for our country.

Would I insult, ostracize, or attack someone who kneels during our National Anthem or fails to rise, remove a hat, or place a hand over his or heart? Absolutely not. Patriotism comes from the heart and soul, and it is not up to any of us to judge others in terms of how they choose to honor (or dishonor) our country. If we start casting judgments on behavior, we are no better than a totalitarian country.

HATE HAS NO HOME AROUND HERE

In suburban America—and in some communities around the world—you may have seen signs in front of homes on front lawns that offer the message: "Hate Has No Home Here." The blue sign includes the American flag in a heart, along with the statement in six languages: English, Hebrew, Arabic, Spanish, Korean, and Urdu. I'm always a bit suspicious of what's lurking behind posters of this nature and decided to do a little digging to determine whether this is legitimate or some form of cultish propaganda.

Well, my research seems to have proven conclusive: The poster and its message are both authentic, and there doesn't appear to be any kind of sinister agenda behind it. It means what it says: *Hate Has No Home Here.* In thinking about it, I'm proud to have the American flag be a part of this— and you should be, too. In my opinion, understanding and acceptance of others plays a major role in American patriotism.

The origins of this poster may be traced back to North

Park, IL in Fall 2016. The residents of this town wanted a slogan to hang in their windows that would counter the intolerance spreading around the community as a result of campaign discussions surrounding immigration. A third grader originated the phrase, which gradually began to catch on.

Not long thereafter, at O'Hare Airport in Chicago, Adin Bendat-Appell—a nine-year-old Jewish boy wearing a yarmulke—perched on his father's shoulders and proudly held up a handwritten sign with the words "Hate Has No Home Here." A photographer happened to catch the moment when a seven-year-old Muslim girl named Meryem Yildirim sat on her father's shoulders and waved a reflective sign back to the Jewish father and son that said, quite simply, "Love."

The photo went viral in the United States and around the world. Designer Steven Luce created the now famous blue poster design with the phrase and the flag, and the rest has become ingrained in our culture.

Some people scratch their heads, react with suspicion, or somehow think it's "un-American" when they see this poster on a front lawn or in a home window. Personally, I think this is patriotism as its best: There is nothing whatsoever objectionable about it, unless you disagree with the message which, to me, is suggestive of some measure of intolerance, as well as a lack of American patriotism.

I'm not suggesting every home must carry this sign, but I do believe that its positive messaging is important. *Hate* is *not* any part of American patriotism, especially if involves political party, skin color, country of origin, religious belief, sexual preference, or any other distinctive factor that makes each one of us human. If you are an American citizen, you have the power within you to be an American patriot. Save the hatred for those who deserve it, such as terrorist organizations and other groups that would do away with personal freedom and liberty and seek to harm American citizens.

HOW WE CAN RE-INSTILL PATRIOTISM
IN AMERICAN POLITICS

While campaigning, Donald Trump had a vague semblance of the right idea in terms of building a supportive base around certain patriotic ideas. The problem, as stated repeatedly throughout this book, is that the messaging (i.e., "Make America Great Again") and symbols (i.e., the red hat) were divisive and offended many true-blue American citizens. To this day, President Trump seems completely oblivious with regard to how he has distorted patriotism to serve his political ambitions and lust for power.

Every politician and his or her supporters want to win an election. They also hope to push their respective agendas once officially in office. That's fine. Voters always have their say and determine who holds the offices that determine such things. But I fear that the 2016 Trump Presidential campaign—as well as his rallies that followed after he took office—encouraged *negative* patriotism and incentivized hatred and bigotry in a way that has become detrimental to genuine American patriotism. It has made many Americans on both sides of the political spectrum uncomfortable with, and mistrustful of, our President, his administration, and the government in general.

We've all, therefore, had to seriously question what being a patriot really means in this day and age. Some radicals feel patriotism is something that can only be exclusively owned by supporters of the current President. They feel you are "either with us or against us." Many Republicans are just "along for the ride"; they are thankful to the President when his agenda happens to work in their favor, especially when it seems to support a strong economy and/or tough immigration laws. Still, there are others who think the ends do not justify the means when it comes to tax laws that benefit the wealthy and immigration laws that put children in cages; all too often they choose to stand silently on the sidelines or else step down from office and recede into the background.

Where does everyone else fit in? If a Democrat or Republican dislikes the President but feels a sense of patriotism, why is it so difficult for him or her to raise an American flag? How can we remove this stigma and restore a sense of national pride for everyone?

There are, of course, those who will always roll their eyes when it comes to any form of patriotism. They think it's a bunch of malarkey or simply view it as cliché or passé to demonstrate patriotism. Well, let's see what we can do to try to repair all of this damage!

Jim's Fifteen New Rules of Patriotism

1. No one can dictate who is or who isn't an American patriot.

2. Individuals of any party—except those who preach hate or intolerance—can be deemed a patriot.

3. Americans of any race, creed, color, religious belief, or sexual preference can be considered a patriot.

4. You do not have to agree with political leaders who are currently in power in order to be worthy of being a patriot.

5. Every American has a patriotic right to express his or her political views, as long as it does not incite or spread hate or violence.

6. You cannot force someone else into becoming a patriot; this is an individual decision.

7. You cannot dictate *how* a person is a patriot; this is also an individual decision.

8. The colors of our flag—red, white, and blue in combination—are the only colors representing American patriotism.

9. Vote! The power to elect good people who represent all Americans is in your hands.

10. Help a veteran: This can involve a lot more than "thanking" a vet (which is also a nice thing to do). You can donate to a veteran's organization or offer assistance to a specific veteran, such as delivering groceries to him or her.

11. Serve on a jury: Like voting, this is a right and privilege. Most people see it as just an inconvenience; however, a right to a fair trial among one's peers is an important part of the American justice system.

12. Buy American products: We've gone away from this over the years, but we want the factories and warehouses to be on American soil and run by American workers. We can do this! (More on this to come in Principle #9.)

13. Teach your children: Every American child should know American history, especially facts about how the country was founded, how our government is structured, and what our famous leaders and citizens have accomplished.

14. Soak in all viewpoints: It may be difficult, but I encourage everyone to read and digest the news from all sides of the political spectrum—left, right, and everything sideways and in the middle. Caution: Be discerning about what you believe and trust: The truth matters!

15. Visit historic sites and memorials: This can include Revolutionary War and Civil War battlegrounds (such as the Freedom in Trail in Boston, MA and Gettysburg National Park in Gettysburg, PA); museums (such as the Smithsonian Museum of American History in Washington, DC); famous homes (such as George Washington's Mount Vernon in Mount Vernon, Virginia); and other important sites (such as the Liberty Bell, located in Independence National Historical Park in Philadelphia, PA).

A FEW NOTES ABOUT PATRIOTIC SONGS

I suppose virtually any tune can be made to come across as patriotic with the right words attached to it. The funny thing is that one of the most accepted patriotic songs of the modern era, "Born in the USA," by Bruce Springsteen doesn't qualify at all! Although it was adopted by politicians (such as President Ronald Reagan) and is often chanted by large crowds of people as an anthem (largely because of the shouting chorus and the powerful snare drum sound), but the song is actually about a soldier fighting in a war he didn't believe in (Vietnam) and returning home to find his government has abandoned him and he can't land a job. (I would repeat the lyrics here—the meaning of which are as plain as day—except for limitations on permissions.) But trust me: While this might be an excellent song, it is not patriotic at all; in reality, it's a poetic diatribe against the American governmental war machine. Similarly, "American Woman," by Canadian band The Guess Who, has been mistaken as a patriotic (or perhaps sex-oriented) song, but the American woman in question is Lady Liberty, and the song's intent was to make a sly statement against America's involvement in Vietnam.

We all know older standards such as "The Star-Spangled Banner," "America the Beautiful," "This Land Is Your Land," and "God Bless America" (or at least think we do), but what are some genuine, enjoyable patriotic songs from recent years? As it happens, there are many that will cause you to raise your chest high with pride!

Jim's Top Twelve Patriotic Songs

1. "City of New Orleans," by Willie Nelson (written by Steve Goodman)

2. "America the Beautiful," by Ray Charles (written by Samuel A. Ward)

3. "This Land is Your Land," by Woody Guthrie

4. "Take Me Home, Country Roads," by John Denver

5. "The Battle Hymn of the Republic," by Whitney Houston (written by Julia Ward Howe)

6. "Pink Houses," by John Mellencamp

7. "American Land," by Bruce Springsteen

8. "The Hammer Song," by The Weavers (written by Pete Seeger and Lee Hayes)

9. "Georgia on My Mind," by Ray Charles (written by Hoagy Carmichael)

10. "American Pie," by Don McLean

11. "Living in America," by James Brown (written by Dan Hartman)

12. "Ragged Old Flag," by Johnny Cash

Of course, if you are in the mood for popular renditions of the classics, try playing these at your next July 4th party:

- "The Star-Spangled Banner," by Jimi Hendrix

- "America the Beautiful," by Aretha Franklin

- "God Bless America," by Generald Wilson

- "This Land Is Your Land," by Peter, Paul, and Mary

PATRIOTIC FILMS THAT STAND THE TEST OF TIME

Any list of favorite patriotic films is going to be a matter of individual taste and preference, so I've done my best to cull the most exhaustive list possible while including a range of genres: war films, historic depictions, dramas, action flicks, and even one science fiction film. You have nothing to lose by binge-watching these with the entire family on Memorial Day, President's Day, or July 4th (if you don't happen to be a fan of fireworks or large barbeques).

Jim's Top Twenty
Most Inspiring Patriotic Films

1. *Saving Private Ryan* (1998, starring Tom Hanks)

2. *Apollo 13* (1995, starring Tom Hanks, Bill Paxton, Kevin Bacon, and Ed Harris)

3. *Patton* (1970, starring George C. Scott)

4. *Twelve O'Clock High* (1949, starring Gregory Peck)

5. *Mr. Smith Goes to Washington* (1939, starring James Stewart, Jean Arthur, and Claude Rains)

6. *Captain America: The First Avenger* (2011, starring Chris Evans)

7. *United 93* (2006, starring Christian Clemenson, Cheyenne Jackson, David Alan Basche, et. Al.)

8. *To Kill a Mockingbird* (1962, starring Gregory Peck)

9. *Yankee Doodle Dandy* (1942, starring James Cagney)

10. *Top Gun* (1986, starring Tom Cruise)

11. *The Right Stuff* (1983, starring Ed Harris and Scott Glenn)

12. *Lincoln* (2012, starring Daniel Day-Lewis)

13. *The American President* (1995, starring Michael Douglas and Annette Bening)

14. *Twelve Angry Men* (1957, starring Henry Fonda)

15. *Miracle* (2004, starring Kurt Russell)

16. *Air Force One* (1997, starring Harrison Ford)

17. *Glory* (1989, starring Matthew Broderick, Denzel Washington, and Morgan Freeman)

18. *The Patriot* (2000, starring Mel Gibson)

19. *Sands of Iwo Jima* (1949, starring John Wayne)

20. *Independence Day* (1999, starring Will Smith, Bill Pullman, and Jeff Goldblum)

Now that you are feeling inspired, comfortable, and patriotic, you are ready to advance to brass tacks about capitalism and money, topics that are essential to *Broken America*—but never at the expense of the other nine Principles.

PRINCIPLE #9: *Capitalism and Money*

Capitalism works.

—Michael Bloomberg, Former Mayor, New York City

Big government or small government?

Use tax money to feed the people and build communities OR to lower corporate tax rates to build business and boost the economy?

Invest money, save money, print money, borrow money, lend money, donate money, hand out money, horde money, exchange money, spend money, waste money, ...

There are many controversies involved with money—and an unlimited number of things you can do with it. As the saying goes, it's what "makes the world go round." A windfall of money can be a wonderful thing for everyone, or it can create a greedy society consisting of *haves* vs. *have nots*. A lack of money—in the form of Recession or Depression—is bad for everyone.

We are a proud capitalist Democracy. We love it when it works in our favor and detest it when our bank accounts and IRA funds head south. America struggles every single day determining the right balance between the needs of the people vs. the needs of our economy. We especially grapple with the role of government programs, bailouts, and debt.

Even Republicans—who traditionally loathe big government, tax hikes, increased debt, and free rides from the government—are more than willing to embrace government funds when the real estate bubble bursts, the market tumbles, or a health pandemic wreaks havoc on public health and our nation's economy.

The reality is that strong government must be in place at all times or our nation fails to function: no military, no local police, no firefighters, no bridges/tunnels, no sewage systems, no parks, no government sites, and on and on. We all care deeply when those things are at risk and flounder, but where does all of the money come from to support them?

This begs the next question: *Is everyone always half right and half wrong with how our government spends our money?*

A CAPITAL IDEA

Interestingly, Adam Smith—who is widely considered the "father of capitalism"—was not an economist, but rather, an 18th century Scottish philosopher. In 1776, coincidentally the year of America's Independence, Smith's influential book, *An Inquiry into the Nature and Causes of the Wealth of Nations* (often shortened to *The Wealth of Nations*), was published. Among other things, Smith put forth the belief in what is known as *free markets*, essentially meaning that people and businesses are motivated by their own self-interests (i.e., directed by their own prosperity). Dumbed down, this means government should not regulate national and international commerce; competition would dictate its own boundaries.

Investopedia.com defines modern capitalism as follows: "…an economic system in which private individuals or businesses own capital goods. The production of goods and services is based on supply and demand in the general market—known as a market economy—rather than through central planning—known as a planned economy or command economy…."

There is a lot of good that comes out of American capitalism: When people spend their hard-earned money on wants and needs, companies offer and produce more to fill the increased demand and the nation prospers. We build more, enjoy a higher standard of living, increase opportunities for future generations and, hopefully, have greater means to help those in need.

During the height of the Reagan and Clinton presidencies, as two prominent examples, the American economy flourished and people felt optimistic about our country's future. We felt so comfortable and strong that we experienced a sense of renewed national pride about where we were headed and believed we were capable of accomplishing anything. To many, an economic boom is a source of patriotism which, as stated in the previous Principle, is most certainly a wonderful thing.

However, we must look ourselves in the mirror and challenge ourselves to answer these questions: *Who benefits the most during such prosperous times and who suffers the most? Is the economy fair and working for everyone? What is the true cost to American citizens at all economic levels?*

As we progress through this Principle, you will find that I believe in the following: Capitalism works, but *balance* and *common sense* must prevail when it comes to managing it properly in our Democracy. Shutting down government programs that feed the homeless is not the answer; nor is creating a Socialist society in which we hand over our life savings to the government.

We tend to get in trouble when we tip the scale too far one way or the other: Either we become selfish and a select few hoard the riches or we overtax people and business, which limits spending. When it comes to this Principle, *Broken America* requires threading the needle and finding just the right middle ground.

DEREGULATION: WHAT COULD POSSIBLY GO WRONG?

Obviously, there exists plenty of government regulation in today's American capitalism, much of which is imperative and should not ever be up for debate. If, for example, a company producing a certain type of plastic were to freely introduce chemicals into the air and water of an entire community, what do you suppose might happen?

Oh, wait. This *did* happen. Between 1951 and 2003, plastic manufacturer DuPont released 1.7 million pounds of Perfluorooctanoic acid (also known as PFOA or C-8) into the town of in Parkersburg, West Virginia. As a result, people became ill and animals perished by the droves. Lawsuits were filed and won to the tune of $671 million, though DuPont denied responsibility on the record. The story became the subject of the 2019 film *Dark Waters*, which starred Mark Ruffalo.

Were any lessons learned from this calamity? Somehow, I don't think they have completely sunk in. When the American economy is booming and everything seems fine and dandy, the natural human inclination is to pull out all stops to boost the stock market and improve the GDP (Gross Domestic Product) even more. America is all about super-sizing, right? One way that Presidential administrations accomplish this is through *deregulations*, which may come in the form of repealing existing policy; or delaying, if not rejecting, approvals on proposed regulations.

Allow me to make this perfectly clear: If a regulation is outdated, adds unnecessarily to big government, or is simply too strict and impedes business, then yes, absolutely: Let's amend it or roll it back entirely.

However, when such actions jeopardize public health and safety, we are going backwards in terms of American progress. President Trump's administration has been reckless with this power, forever altering the course of the government's ability to help protect the people as necessary—especially when it comes to environmental issues, such as protecting the air we breathe and ensuring clean water. (The Trump deregulation tally is being monitored on a regular basis by Brookings, a D.C. nonprofit; the site may be found here: https://www.brookings.edu/interactives/tracking-deregulation-in-the-trump-era/.) We will only know the toll of this massive volume of deregulation until after it's too late—when people become ill or suffer injuries from things that had previously been deterred. I sincerely hope no one benefits at someone else's expense, but time will tell....

AMERICA'S DEBT: NO ONE CAN COUNT THIS HIGH

One of President Donald Trump's campaign promises back in 2016 was to reduce America's debt. Shortly after he took office, he passed a budget that would increase the national debt by $8.3 trillion over eight years. In spring 2020, in response to the Recession and unprecedented unemployment caused by the COVID-19 epidemic, several trillion dollars in relief for citizens and businesses were added on top of that.

Most worrisome about the above is the $500 billion being handed over to corporations, including the grounded airline industry. *How can we be assured that this money will go toward keeping the businesses afloat and paying employees, rather than lining the pockets of corporate executives?* The answer is that there aren't any assurances whatsoever. In fact, as I write this, President Trump has fired Glenn A. Fine—the well-respected, bipartisan acting Inspector General who headed the watchdog panel overseeing how bailout money is spent—without rhyme or reason. The only possible explanation is that Trump doesn't want anyone sniffing around where all of that money ends up going.

And...wait just one minute here. All of the other payments to individuals and small businesses are seemingly well and good on the surface, but isn't the Republican party supposedly the *conservative* party that hates national debt and governmental overspending? I'm not remotely suggesting the 2020 bailouts were unnecessary or that Trump was even responsible for it. (They were bipartisan and passed by the Congress and Senate. It's a miracle—at long last, the two sides came together and agreed on something!) I'm simply throwing out the questions: *How long can America possibly sustain itself with such insurmountable debt on it shoulders and the 8.3 trillion from Trump's budget already accumulating, including money spent on a wasteful border wall?* Last I heard, organizations that don't pay their bills or debt end up with the lights turned off.

Somewhere along the way—decades before the Coronavirus bailout—*both parties* have become irresponsible with other people's money—*our* money. It all comes down to years of misspending, misappropriation, and mismanagement. The "too big to fail" concept breeds bad leadership and economic disparity. I believe far more in the notion "too *small* to fail." We *must* support small businesses. Why? Because Americans will feel much greater pride in supporting and cheering their success, employment will rise, and overall spending and investments will increase.

DECISION TIME: THE AMERICAN ECONOMY OR AMERICA'S HEALTH?

The answer to the above heading is pretty clear-cut: The health and safety of our citizens must always come first. Health epidemics don't favor rich capitalists; we are all vulnerable to a contagion. I care deeply about the economy and the health of our nation. Personally, I love making money! But what good is all of that dough if we don't take care of our people and thousands of innocent people get sick and die? I call that grossly irresponsible. First, we must support the people and then—and only then—will we rebound. America has survived wars, famine, depression, and more. Working together, we can survive a health epidemic—can't we?

All it takes for us to overcome the worst circumstances is good, consistent leadership, which we had during the Revolutionary War, the Civil War, and World War II. Unfortunately, during the COVID-19 outbreak of 2020, we had a shortage of this in some pretty high places of government.

On January 22, 2020, President Donald Trump made a statement at the World Economic Forum about COVID-19 and its potential threat. "We have it totally under control," he told CNBC. "It's one person coming in from China, and we have it under control. It's going to be just fine." Over the course of the next few weeks, Trump denied that the virus would be any kind of issue for American citizens, repeatedly stating (and Tweeting) that it was just going to "go away."

Well, this did *not* happen and America ended up being ill-prepared for this pandemic, which is currently ravaging the health of Americans at an unprecedented rate. There aren't enough tests, masks, ventilators, or hospital beds for the health community, patients, and citizens. Americans have been ordered to stay at home to avoid contaminating themselves and others—but all of it feels like too little, too late. The virus has spread like wildfire and already claimed tens of thousands of lives.

In the meantime, several Republican governors—most prominently Ron DeSantis of Florida, where the virus had already been manifesting—were slow to issue stay at home orders for their states. DeSantis didn't start taking action until the end of March 2020 when the virus had already infected 7,000 people and claimed 85 lives in his state. He would have continued to ignore the escalation if state lawmakers on both sides of the aisle hadn't applied significant pressure on him.

What went on here? Did President Trump, Governor DeSantis, and others truly believe the virus wasn't a threat? Did they not realize or care about the impact of their decisions?

Allow me to emphatically underscore this point: *I do not blame President Trump, Governor DeSantis, or anyone else for the virus or its spread in America.* There is no denying America would have been hammered by COVID-19 no matter what controls had been in place.

What I *do* blame them for is choosing economic health over the health of the people. Tests, hospital masks, ventilators, and hospital beds could have been readied back in January when the President first heard the report of the virus. At the same time, American leadership should have looked at what was happening in China and spreading to Europe and prepared the American people for what was to come through education (i.e., social distancing, proper hand washing, etc.). For weeks, the President ignored and/or poo-pooed numbers about the virus and its dangers while blaming Democrats at his rallies, which set the tone for people who believed his fabrications.

He even suggested that a boat docked in San Francisco with some COVID-19 patients should not be allowed to enter because they would impact the numbers. President Trump feared the volume of cases would go up, which would impact the stock market which, in turn, would affect his re-election hopes. A few weeks later, he proposed that Americans would be healthy and ready to celebrate Easter together—an idea that was not shared by a single member of the medical community. On top of that, he demanded flattery and praise from America's governors in exchange for much-needed supplies to help their states during the time of crisis.

And there's more! He refuses to wear a mask (to prevent the spread of the disease) when around other people because he regards it as a sign of weakness. On the contrary, wearing a mask is exactly what he *should* do to lead by example, as it would help remove any stigma associated with a mask and educate the people on how we can best protect ourselves.

To sum it all up: Our President chose the economy and his vanity over the health of American citizens. As of this date (spring 2020), many Americans continue to believe early tirades from Trump (at his rallies) and certain Fox news commentators characterizing the epidemic as a hoax created by Democrats. How are we supposed to end this epidemic if we listen to greedy politicians over the medical community, spread harmful lies, and continue the political spit-fighting?

Yes, we will overcome the COVID-19 pandemic—but it is the perfect example of why empathy is such an important Leadership attribute of a president (see Principle #2). We pay a steep price for having voted in a president who chooses power, votes, and money over the health of our citizens.

THE SYSTEM IS LITERALLY BROKE—HERE'S A WAY TO FIX IT

Health care. Infrastructure. The tax system.

Let's face it: If the government is involved in an initiative, something is certainly broken within it. Everyone seems to have an idea of what to do with taxpayer dollars, yet rarely does it seem to amount to real solutions. We have so much corruption and mismanagement in government it's a wonder anything ever gets done. We have thousands of distressed urban and rural communities in our country in which jobs, health care, and basic food and other necessities are difficult to come by. Whereas the average life span for most of the world is increasing, Americans are actually heading in the other direction when it comes to longevity.

I have two solutions for this broken socio-economic situation. The first is something I mentioned in Principle Six. As a reminder: The Tax Cuts Jobs Act of 2017 (TCJA) includes a piece of legislation that can help revitalize these communities: investing in Qualified Opportunity Zones (QOZs) with Qualified Opportunity Zones (QOFs). It's a rare opportunity for investors to save money by deferring capital gains earnings. They would roll the money over into a QOF, which would improve neighborhoods that have been down-trending. Ultimately, they would see a profit on their investments as well.

As outlined in my previous book, *Opportunity Investing*, QOFs provide investors with the ability to unite their heads and hearts and make a genuine difference without it smacking of "charity." You can invest in real estate (i.e., everything from homes and offices to bowling alleys and concert centers to golf courses and waterparks); to investment sectors (i.e., energy, industrials, technology); community services (i.e., schools, hospitals); and more. We can also do something to repair and rebuild our crumbling infrastructure. You can invest in QOFs in order to: sustain bridges, tunnels, or parks; or improve water, sanitation, and transportation services.

That's not all. The next big thing in innovation could happen in one of those QOZs simply by investing in the right funds. These communities are the perfect sites for business accelerators and incubators to help foster brilliant new ideas, which are developed in garages and basements every day in our country.

There is no risk, as investors would otherwise be paying taxes on their capital gains earnings. By the same token, the government doesn't need to raise taxes or spend a dime. Once the funds are in place and active, the businesses and jobs will flood into these communities, the affordable housing market will soar, and the neighborhoods themselves will benefit from the infrastructure improvements.

What do we have to lose? Nothing whatsoever.

LET'S MAKE IT GREAT IN AMERICA AGAIN

The second idea for restoring America's economic stature is to bring back President Ronald Reagan's slogan "Made in America" and blend it with the Trump campaign slogan "Make America Great Again" to create the following: "Let's Make *It Great in America* Again." By merging these two phrases, we are conveying a patriotic message and uniting all political parties at the same time.

Why *wouldn't* we wish to set the stage for all of our products to once again be made in America? We want and need the jobs right here on our soil. For too long, product creation and manufacturing have been outsourced overseas, as have IT and Helpdesk support in a number of different industries. Yes, it can be a lot cheaper, cost-efficient, and simpler for America to farm out certain tasks—but what has the long-term toll of this been to American workers and on our economy?

Justifiably or not, many Republicans are concerned that immigrants (especially Mexicans) are taking jobs away from American workers. Here are the facts: Prior to the COVID-19 outbreak, 14.3 million American jobs were outsourced versus approximately six million unemployed. Wow! Instead of worrying about the immigrants, why not hold businesses accountable for keeping the jobs right here in the USA?

Now is precisely the right time to start planning it. With the COVID-19 virus spreading throughout the United States, it is estimated that unemployment might reach as high as 32%. When the situation eventually improves, the smoke clears, and things return to some semblance of business as usual with people seeking to return to work, why wouldn't companies want to take this opportunity to reboot their operations? With this in mind, couldn't we establish a lower cost of product creation and services here in America as we ramp back up?

Once such a restart has been initiated and we have a clean slate, I would be in favor of offering tax incentives to small and large companies alike to incentivize them to transfer operations that had been parked offshore and plant them on American soil. Such an act would undoubtedly turn around unemployment, reinvigorate businesses, and bolster the economy. At that point, Americans will once again feel patriotic about buying home-grown products because contributing to this effort helps the cause to get our country back on its feet. If this ends up being the new interpretation of "America First," I am all in favor of it!

Of course, we have a lot of work to do in order to help our nation return to a state of good health and financial prosperity. Every American must stop the political bickering and work together, so we may learn from the COD-19 crisis and prepare well ahead for the next calamity, whatever it might be.

What we do know for sure: A strong economy is absolutely critical to sustaining America's future. But we can never again—not for one single second—choose money over the health of American citizens. Though the data is only preliminary as of this writing, statistics are already showing that black and Hispanic populations have been at higher risk of dying from COVID-19, possibly due to a combination of economic conditions, lack of availability of medical care, and pre-existing conditions in their communities. It is tragic that politicians—who have much greater access to health care than minorities living in distressed areas—make decisions that are a matter of life and death on everyone's behalf.

When the medical community says there is an imminent threat, the financial and political communities must listen, take a backseat, and do what is right to ensure the public's safety. The same people who insist upon business as usual during a health crisis may someday find themselves in the undesirable position of having to care for a loved one who becomes ill. No one wants to see this. We must *always* choose health over money. If we don't, precious few people will remain to spend anything.

With that in mind, let's turn to a subject that is far less contentious and much more upbeat: *compromise*.

PRINCIPLE #10: *Compromise*

Fight as hard as you can, and then
understand there's going to have to be
some kind of reasonable compromise.

—*Andrew Cuomo, Governor of New York*

It may strike some people as odd that I count *compromise* as one of the ten Principles. Not only do I consider this art form critical in relation to politics, I have saved it specially as the final Principle to conclude this book.

Why? I believe that being able to negotiate skillfully is one of the most valuable assets we have when developing relationships. It is relevant to all kinds of relationships, in all kinds of settings. We are carrying out negotiations all of the time. My intent is for this Principle to be of value for both politicians involved in disputes and negotiations, as well as for citizens brave enough to tackle sensitive political discourse with others—including friends and family members who may belong to opposing parties.

Let's come back full circle to our Founding Fathers. I would go as far as saying that compromise was perhaps the most essential element in colonial politics. The Constitutional Convention stretched out over a three-and-a half-month period with many differences of opinion and heated arguments. Cooler heads, such as George Washington and Benjamin Franklin, prevailed in order to support the greater good. If not for them, the American government—as imperfect as it may now seem at times—would never have come to fruition. The late Presidential advisor and NATO ambassador David M. Abshire put it this way: "The Founders were warriors for their cause, but whenever possible, civility was their martial art of choice—respect, collaboration, and compromise over a saber, musket, and cannon. That's why the Founders would find the claim that 'politics is about winning, not about compromise' to be a false choice. Politics is about winning, but compromise is how you win."

Today, people are out way too much to "win" and "win big"—meaning, everything must be on their own terms. It's "all or nothing" or there is no deal; be prepared to "walk away," they say. With this mindset, no matter what the outcome, it's lose-lose for all parties involved.

The fact of the matter is this: If we cannot come to a compromise, we have done a poor job. This doesn't just hold true in politics. We negotiate every day at work and in our personal lives, yet often become too stubborn and fail to compromise in those areas as well.

Perhaps some of the failure resides in a misunderstanding of the meaning behind the word *compromise*. A lot of people think the word means you have given up on something important to keep the peace. Rather than accept this type of thinking, I would suggest focusing on the positive and the mutual end result of the negotiation: *the solution*.

I define compromise along the lines of the following: "An ability to listen to two sides in a disagreement or dispute, concede points on both sides, and arrive at an amicable agreement that satisfies both parties in order to achieve a common goal."

The above definition accentuates the positive aspects of compromise, not the negative possible connotation of having been compromised. It also ensures that all parties have a stated common goal. I believe this is always going to be the case; somehow, some way there is always a common goal. If both parties start with that and then backtrack, the question of "How do we get there?" becomes a lot easier.

DON'T CO-OPT—COOPERATE

Some level of compromise is always needed in order for parties to reach an agreement. The first important step in this process involves establishing cooperation. If it appears you are out solely for yourself and your own interests, the negotiation will fail and everyone will lose. Here are a few general pointers on cooperation:

- *Try looking at the situation from the other person's point of view.* Use your imagination to step into the other person's shoes.

- *Open up.* Take a calculated risk by expressing how you feel and what you want.

- *Earn trust.* Demonstrate that you believe the other side has good intentions.

- *Keep in contact.* Do not allow yourself to avoid discussing thorny issues.

- *Recognize that people vary in their needs.* People require different amounts of closeness, silence (to express their feelings or let off steam), sharing, and independence. Allow time for everyone to breathe and process information.

- *Be clear and transparent about what you want.* Don't play games or attempt to use reverse psychology. Not only don't these tactics work, they come across as manipulative.

- *Respect the other side's point of view.* Disrespect only causes people to dig in harder against you.

DEAL OR NO DEAL? PLAY THE RELATIONSHIP GAME, NOT THE NEGOTIATION GAME

The bottom line in all negotiations is that everyone is free to decide to walk away without a deal in place. This happens all of the time in politics for many reasons, but mainly due to the following circumstances leaders face: 1) They are representing the assets and rights of citizens; 2) They are often under significant political pressure; 3) They seek to get re-elected; and 4) They can't get out of the way of their own egos and seem weak by not getting all of their demands.

This begs the question: In politics, is the adage "No deal is better than a bad deal" true? Sometimes *yes*, and sometimes *no*. Every day, politicians must decide if their end games are worth a few sacrifices here and there. But are they playing hardball and holding out for the right reasons and the best objectives?

In most cases, "all or nothing" ultimatums are a poor ploy when it comes to political engagements, which can impact thousands of citizens. Walking away is a pretty major step to take. It's also a great risk. It can become a relationship-buster with no turning back. Once a politician storms out of a negotiation, it becomes nearly impossible to return to the table because neither side wants to lose face at that stage. (Once again, that fragile ego surfaces.) Then the next time that hot-headed politician needs something from the opposition, either he or she won't get the time of day or else will be on the receiving end of a brusque walk-out, due to spite.

In politics, there is always plenty of room for negotiation. Everyone in a relationship has something to gain by presenting new options to continue the dialogue. In the long run, this is the most satisfactory way of relating. Finding ways to work together with other people can make things happen that otherwise could not. A friend of mine had a great Uncle Moe who happened to be an attorney. During intense legal negotiations, Uncle Moe used this wonderful catch phrase: "For every problem there's a solution."

It is important for politicians to consider ways in which everyone searches for options and solutions to problems at the same time to boost the relationship, thereby earning trust. All parties involved benefit from creative discussion, rather than posturing and digging in deep on a position.

The "I win, you lose" scenario is not only intrinsically unfair, it ends up becoming a long-term disadvantage. The losing side draws away from you and feels burned, which will not bode well during future negotiations. On the flip side, "you win: I lose" won't work, either, as then you risk being treated like a doormat in the future. Of course, "lose, lose"—meaning no deal for anyone—means a future relationship will likely be untenable.

REACHING ACROSS THE AISLE IS NOT A SIGN OF WEAKNESS

There are a couple of fallacies about business and political relationships that need to be swatted away. The first: "A relationship that needs working at is not worth having." It is actually quite the contrary; work is essential to building and retaining a relationship. All concerned must be committed to making a concerted effort.

The problem may reside in any usage of the word "work." By definition, *work* smacks of arduous labor. Instead, we should replace it with the word *adaptation* when it comes to negotiating, as it is far more positive and sounds like less of a chore.

The second phrase: "You should know how I feel." This is an absurd phrase. Unless we are telepathic aliens, it's simply not logical for anyone to assume someone knows our heart or mind. By assuming the other person should know how you feel, you are being passive-aggressive and withholding valuable information that could help all sides. In this scenario, it is easy for false conclusions to be drawn and for people to take things personally when they were not intended that way. Human behavior can be truly subjective: preoccupation may be confused with indifference; frustration may be mixed up with anger and hostility; and so on.

When the arms are extended across the aisle, it is in everyone's interests to be as transparent and straightforward as possible (without, of course, giving anything away that could jeopardize the negotiation) and to not assume anything about the other side. These two questions are always good to ask: "What are you thinking?" and "How do you feel about that?" You'll be surprised by what you hear back.

JIM'S FIFTEEN SUREFIRE RULES OF ANY NEGOTIATION

I've been through many negotiations in my time and, as a result of trial and error, have found that the secret to a happy, mutually beneficial resolution is obtaining compromise through the following fifteen rules:

Rule #1: Never have your mind made up.

In their classic book on negotiation *Getting to Yes*, authors Roger Fisher and William Ury state: "An open mind is not an empty one." If you have an open mind as you practice active listening—as described in Principle #7—you might find that you agree with one or two points made by the other party. That is a good thing. It provides you with areas you can concede to add balance against the places where you can't. It takes a big person to see another person's point of view enough to change her mind on the spot—a fact that will earn great deal of trust and respect.

Rule #2: Find out what everyone wants.

Relationships are systems, which means that you obscure half your vision if you think only about what you want. You need to think both *about the other party's perspective, as well as your own.*

Rule #3: Search for common ground.

Common ground is useful as a starting point. It demonstrates the parties aren't so far apart and have the capability of reaching an agreement.

Rule #4: State your opinion.

While you want to engage in active listening and respectfully acknowledge other speakers, you are also entitled to state your personal opinion when you have the floor. You are allowed to be candid and disagree, as long you maintain professional body language, keep your emotions in check, and don't attack others (including through sarcasm). You should never agree with something when you don't. You may decide to concede the point as part of your compromise, but you must hold true to your beliefs.

Rule #5: Stay concrete and factual.

You will lose the interest and support of the room if you exaggerate or veer off on a tangent. Stick to the facts, Jack.

Rule #6: Don't talk too much.

Never talk over other people or usurp discussion time. Give everyone equal opportunity to speak. In a political debate, candidate performance is often measured at least in part by how many minutes he or she spoke. The opposite holds true in a conversation requiring compromise. The fewer words, the better.

Rule #7: Help others speak up.

If a person at the table seems reserved and quiet, consciously ask her what she thinks. She may have a valuable suggestion or had been holding something back. You want everyone to be comfortable enough to participate and make suggestions.

Rule #8: Always take input seriously.

No matter how you feel about someone else's statement, do not discount or ridicule it. It's virtually impossible to walk a remark back once a person feels insulted.

Rule #9: Keep tabs on what has been said.

Be sure to clarify what the other person means and what you mean. Whether people agree or disagree with each other's remarks, don't allow any perspectives to get lost. Make sure the group has responded in some way to everything. When necessary, repeat or summarize statements to keep them fresh and show you have been paying attention.

Rule #10: Build on what the other person says.

Instead of reacting and saying "no" the instant you hear

something you don't like, look for what you can accept and start with a "yes." This takes you out of conflict mode and straight into negotiations.

Rule #11: Cut out the blame.

The mindset should always be that there are differing points of view, rather than one wrong one and one right one. Instead of focusing on who might be at fault, think in terms of shared responsibility. This may sound overly optimistic or naïve; there are occasions when a person truly is to blame. However, a flurry—or even a dusting—of accusations serve only to make people defensive.

Rule #12: Bottle up the insults.

Some insults, such as name-calling or negatively characterizing a person's point of view (i.e., "pig-headed," stubborn," etc.), are obvious, whereas others are not. You can't always be aware of another person's sensitivities, so you must tread lightly. Even remarking upon another person's position as "illogical" may be heard as something derogatory. It is best to avoid making any offensive or irritating comments, even if you believe one has been fired off at you.

Rule #13: Watch out for escalation.

In any negotiation, it's possible for tensions to mount and instantly spiral out of control. When you sense this, call for an immediate break so everyone has a chance to cool off before resuming the discussion.

Rule #14: Broaden the basis of the negotiation.

A negotiation often flounders because it all hinges on one thing. For example, a political disagreement on updating a zoning law may hinge entirely on the geographical location of enforcement. Instead of focusing on this aspect, a politician might point out how the new law would positively benefit small businesses within the territory, as well as contribute to the town's overall prosperity.

Rule #15: Look for opportunities to trade.

Identify the issues that are most important to the other party and see if you can find a way to address them. In such circumstances, you are stripping away all of the smaller items and boiling them down to one central "give" that enables compromise to take place.

Unfortunately, as we all know all too well, even the best rules, strategies, and tactics don't always pan out. This is when you need to call upon a lifeline to keep the negotiations going.

WE CAN WORK IT OUT—WITH A LITTLE HELP FROM AN OBJECTIVE PARTY

Sometimes an objective moderator or mediator can help two parties arrive at necessary compromise before things have a chance to become heated. Both sides of the discussion must mutually agree to this individual in advance of the meeting; there shouldn't be any surprises.

There are distinctions between a moderator and mediator, of course. A good moderator will keep the discussion moving, enable all points to be properly aired, and ensure everyone makes a contribution. A strong mediator will not only manage the conversation but will also help the parties find common ground and places where equivalent compromises can be made.

THE MORAL IMPERATIVE

In a fascinating paper entitled "Possible Ways to Promote Compromise," Brian Tomasik presents an intellectual treatise on ways to join people together with different belief systems through the art of compromise. Essentially, we all hold different moral views associated with our group associations that prevent us from being able to relate to and accept beliefs that fall outside our frame of reference. In a specific religion, for example, symbols and rituals can be as powerful as an "electrical current" to unite and charge a group of people with shared views. I'm not being sarcastic when I say that this type of group power exists in politics and even in sports fandom, where symbols (team colors, logos, and even mascots) represent the collective.

If everything is handled correctly according to all of the suggestions in this chapter, yet the parties still fail to connect and compromise, is the deal kaput? How can two diametrically opposed philosophies overcome "us vs. them" thinking and ever hope to find a compromise?

The answer is an emphatic "yes." Let's consider a sports analogy brought up earlier in this book. Fan support for a major league baseball team can occasionally get pretty fierce, go overboard, and maybe even lead to a physical brawl under the right circumstances (especially when alcohol is involved). Do you think New York Yankees fans and Boston Red Sox fans will ever join a group hug and compromise their team loyalty? Highly unlikely. But they do share at least one major thing in common: the love of baseball.

When it comes to politics, we all have a distinct commonality: *pride in our country*. Liberals and Conservatives may hash it out on many issues and never budge an inch either way, but both sides can see eye-to-eye on one thing: the love of the United States of America.

I'd like to close this Principle by offering an important, if controversial suggestion. Let's mutually agree to compromise by putting some blinders on about the *why* in order to consider the *what if*? In other words, let's place ourselves inside a utopian scenario to find commonality.

What if…all Americans were to *compromise*? What would be the downside? Absolutely nothing. At last, we would settle on common ground—love of country—and allow the most important points from each side to win the day. I believe this is essential in order for us to re-unify America, don't you agree?

Attention Republicans, Democrats, Conservatives, Liberals, Libertarians, et al: As long as we do not preach hate or violence, we are all American patriots and we are all part of the same cause. We can work together to find solutions to our differences. All we need to do is come to the table with an open heart and an open mind.

EPILOGUE: *The Future Is Within Our Grasp*

Always vote for principle, although you may
vote alone, and you may cherish
the sweetest reflection that your vote
is never lost.

—*John Quincy Adams, 6th President of the United States*

My fellow Americans: We are at a crossroads in our country. Although we have made it through a Revolutionary War, a Civil War, two World Wars, the Great Depression, the Korean War, the Vietnam War, the Cold War, 9/11, and the 2007-2009 Recession, we may be involved in the greatest crisis our country has faced as a whole. While this work heads off to production and then to the printer, we are all in our homes practicing social distancing to prevent the spread of COVID-19; coping with mass illness and loss; dealing with economic collapse and skyrocketing unemployment; and struggling to maintain our sanity through it all.

Meanwhile, our pre-existing political and socio-economic divide has only been exacerbated by this horrific situation. We can't trust what certain leaders are telling us to do or not do as a result of political pressure; panic about the economy and/or the stock market; or just plain ignorance. Sometimes it seems like we will need nothing short of a miracle to get America back on track.

And yet…miracles can happen. I do not believe that I am preaching "happy talk" when I state that I wholeheartedly believe we are capable of getting through this bleak period and, ultimately, restoring America's true greatness and civility as a world leader. But it requires the complete cooperation of every leader and citizen to embrace the ten principles in this book as our *Next Big Thing in Politics*: *Vision; Leadership; Truth-Seeking; Courage; Integrity; Tolerance and Equality; Respect; Patriotism; Capitalism and Money; and Compromise.*

One leader cannot accomplish this alone. Nor can just a village. It requires a commitment from every single patriotic American to bury their muskets, as it were, and agree that, while we may never see eye-to-eye on all of the issues, we all long for the same things: love, honor, and prosperity for our country and our commitment to a shared bright future.

Given social distancing norms to avoid the spread of contagion, we cannot seal this agreement with a hug, a handshake, a kiss, or a pact in blood. However, we can do it by cherishing our Constitution, voting worthy leaders into office, celebrating the truth, lowering the temperature on public discourse, and holding both the media and government accountable for their words and actions.

To quote President Abraham Lincoln: "The best thing about the future is that it comes one day at a time." There is no better time to start than right this minute.

Let's Make it Great in America Again.

Sources

PREFACE:

https://www.brainyquote.com/quotes/alexander_hamilton_135307

INTRODUCTION:

https://founders.archives.gov/documents/Franklin/01-20-02-0213

https://www.npr.org/2014/11/13/363762677/the-color-of-politics-how-did-red-and-blue-states-come-to-be

https://www.cnn.com/2013/07/27/us/september-11-anniversary-fast-facts/index.html

http://www.john-adams-heritage.com/quotes/

PART ONE:

https://blog.tenthamendmentcenter.com/2017/01/we-have-it-in-our-power-to-begin-the-world-over-again/

https://www.mentalfloss.com/article/57009/30-presidential-nicknames-explained

https://learnodo-newtonic.com/george-washington-accomplishments

https://www.annenbergclassroom.org/resource
/our-constitution/constitution-chapter-1-
constitution-necessary

https://quoteinvestigator.com/tag/
oliver-wendell-holmes/

PART TWO:

http://www.digitalhistory.uh.edu/disp_textbook.
cfm?smtID=3&psid=3943

PRINCIPLE ONE:

https://www.jfklibrary.org/learn/education/teachers/
curricular-resources/elementary-school-curricular-
resources/ask-not-what-your-country-can-do-for-
you?gclid=CjwKCAjwhOD0BRAQEiwAK7JHmK-
Kp8E8d0YI688-5D_QQDAyqExYZJTcCqc0BYr-
mai9GVc5aGMwjlLhoCgbAQAvD_BwE

https://www.heritage.org/commentary/
the-man-who-would-not-be-king

https://www.history.com/news/
abraham-lincoln-house-divided-speech

https://en.wikiversity.org/wiki/
Talk:Albert_Einstein_quote

https://www.presentationmagazine.com/winston-
churchill-speech-we-shall-fight-them-on-the-
beaches-8003.htm

https://www.jfklibrary.org/learn/education/teachers/
curricular-resources/elementary-school-curricular-
resources/ask-not-what-your-country-can-do-for-you

https://en.wikipedia.org/wiki/List_of_U.S._
presidential_campaign_slogans

https://www.vox.com/energy-and-environment/
2019/4/24/18512804/climate-change-united-
states-china-emissions.

https://www.usgs.gov/faqs/how-much-carbon-dioxide-
does-united-states-and-world-emit-each-year-energy-
sources?qt-news_science_products=0#qt-news_
science_products

https://thehill.com/homenews/administration/
457206-top-trump-immigration-official-defends-
public-charge-rule-give-me

PRINCIPLE TWO:

https://quotefancy.com/quote/1325974/John-Stuart-
Mill-A-great-statesman-is-he-who-knows-when-to-
depart-from-traditions-as-well

https://www.npr.org/2016/12/28/506299885/
how-the-donald-trump-cabinet-stacks-up-in-3-charts

https://abcnews.go.com/Politics/trump-calls-
tillerson-dumb-rock-quoted-putin-prepared/
story?id=63202565

https://www.brookings.edu/research/
tracking-turnover-in-the-trump-administration/

https://allauthor.com/quotes/39808/

https://www.washingtonpost.com/opinions/
trust-but-verify-an-untrustworthy-politi-
cal-phrase/2016/03/11/da32fb08-db3b-11e5-891a-
4ed04f4213e8_story.html

https://www.brainyquote.com/quotes/
benito_mussolini_382794

https://twitter.com/veepquotes/status/
473530436229283840?lang=en

https://www.nytimes.com/1973/09/23/archives/
kissinger-sworn-praised-by-nixon-what-america-
means.html

https://www.google.com/search?client=safari&rls=
en&sxsrf=ALeKk03CoHZlJvzjHRDUcdRn_
xETFsWpzA%3A1582298299241&ei=u_
RPXtikDoy-ggfrzILAAw&q=Joe+Biden+Medal+
of+Freedom&oq=Joe+Biden+Medal+of+Free-
dom&gs_l=psy-ab.3..0l3j0i22i30l7.3126.7382..
7632...0.0..0.115.2067.26j1......0....1..gws-wiz
.......35i39j0i131i67j0i273j0i67j0i131
i273j0i20i263j0i131j0i131i67i70i251.
GOS0XrUihAE&ved=0ahUKEwiY7rfA-
OLnAhUMn-AKHWumADgQ4dUDCAo&uact=5

https://www.washingtonpost.com/news/the-fix/
wp/2017/12/20/in-cabinet-meeting-pence-praises-
trump-once-every-12-seconds-for-3-minutes-straight/

https://www.industryweek.com/
the-economy/trade/article/21959071/
december-is-made-in-america-month

https://www.govinfo.gov/content/pkg/STATUTE-100/
pdf/STATUTE-100-Pg4389.pdf

https://quotes.yourdictionary.com/author/
rudy-giuliani/55874

https://www.youtube.com/watch?v=nwL6GWYg34M

https://www.youtube.com/watch?v=kEe7_zgZbuI

https://www.history.com/news/did-marie-antoinette-
really-say-let-them-eat-cake

https://www.saturdayeveningpost.com/2013/06/
lincoln-jokes/

https://www.brainyquote.com/quotes/
ronald_reagan_130243

https://www.quotes.net/quote/13224

https://www.realclearpolitics.com/articles/2008/10/
barack_obama_at_the_al_smith_d.html

https://www.phrases.org.uk/bulletin_board/54/
messages/368.html

https://www.jfklibrary.org/archives/other-resources/
john-f-kennedy-speeches/syracuse-university-
19570603

https://www.powerquotations.com/quote/
   quote-me-as-saying-i

https://www.psychologytoday.com/us/blog/political-
   intelligence/201204/learning-humility-l

https://www.scoopwhoop.com/
   global-leaders-simple-living/

https://www.passiton.com/inspirational-quotes/3617-
   never-look-down-on-anybody-unless-youre-helping

https://www.csmonitor.com/Books/Book-
   Reviews/2017/0623/John-Quincy-Adams-shares-the-
   diary-of-America-s-most-passionate-president

https://www.biography.com/us-president/
   andrew-jackson

https://www.nytimes.com/2007/01/14/weekinreview/
   14green.html?auth=login-email&login=email

https://www.jfklibrary.org/events-and-awards/
   profile-in-courage-award/about-the-book

https://www.cheatsheet.com/culture/presidents-
   with-the-most-unpresidential-personalities-
   including-donald-trump.html/

https://www.brainyquote.com/quotes/
   bruce_lee_378322

PRINCIPLE THREE:

https://www.willrogers.com/quotes

https://www.washingtonpost.com/

https://www.factcheck.org/2020/02/factchecking-trumps-coronavirus-press-conference/

https://www.nytimes.com/interactive/2020/us/coronavirus-us-cases.html

https://www.factcheck.org/2020/02/will-the-new-coronavirus-go-away-in-april/

https://www.rollingstone.com/politics/politics-news/anatomy-of-a-fake-news-scandal-125877/

https://mediabiasfactcheck.com/new-york-times/

https://www.washingtonian.com/2019/10/02/trump-claims-he-invented-the-term-fake-news-an-interview-with-the-guy-who-actually-helped-popularize-it/

PRINCIPLE FOUR:

http://www.quotationspage.com/quote/26626.html

https://www.senate.gov/reference/reference_item/Profiles_In_Courage.html

https://www.washingtonpost.com/

https://www.keepinspiring.me/margaret-thatcher-quotes/

PRINCIPLE FIVE:

https://ministry127.com/resources/illustration/eisenhower-on-leadership

https://www.cbsnews.com/news/richard-burr-coronavirus-kelly-loeffler-dianne-feinstein-james-inhofe-sold-lots-of-stock-virus-fears-started/

https://www.history.com/topics/us-presidents/read-my-lips-no-new-taxes-video

https://www.axios.com/10-big-broken-promises-of-past-presidents-1513301978-5b4fd8ba-a90a-450a-873e-51226c9861c9.html

https://www.nytimes.com/2019/01/11/us/politics/trump-mexico-pay-wall.html

https://www.washingtonpost.com/

PRINCIPLE SIX:

https://www.beliefnet.com/quotes/inspiration/h/henry-david-thoreau/it-is-never-too-late-to-give-up-your-prejudices.aspx

https://www.nbcbayarea.com/news/coronavirus/web-site-launches-to-document-anti-asian-hate-crimes-in-wake-of-covid-19/2258297/

https://www.nbcnews.com/news/us-news/woman-accused-slapping-3-jews-brooklyn-charged-federal-hate-crimes-n1124651

https://www.dailyeasternnews.com/2020/02/21/eastern-responds-to-hate-messages/

https://www.nbcnews.com/news/us-news/hate-crimes-america-spiked-17-percent-last-year-fbi-says-n935711

https://www.justice.gov/hatecrimes/hate-crime-statistics

https://www.jewishvirtuallibrary.org/statistics-on-religious-hate-crimes

https://www.pewsocialtrends.org/2019/04/09/views-of-racial-inequality/

https://www.payscale.com/data/gender-pay-gap

https://www.goodreads.com/quotes/293079-the-only-freedom-which-deserves-the-name-is-that-of

https://www.cnn.com/2017/08/12/us/charlottesville-white-nationalists-rally/index.html

https://www.cnn.com/2017/08/12/politics/trump-statement-alt-right-protests/index.html

https://www.vox.com/2017/8/12/16138358/charlottesville-protests-david-duke-kkk

https://www.brookings.edu/blog/fixgov/2019/08/14/trump-and-racism-what-do-the-data-say/

https://www.pewresearch.org/fact-tank/2019/06/28/
what-we-know-about-illegal-immigration-from-
mexico/

https://www.factcheck.org/2018/06/is-illegal-
immigration-linked-to-more-or-less-crime/

https://www.theatlantic.com/international/archive/
2017/01/trump-immigration-ban-terrorism/514361

White, Ph.D., Jim. *Opportunity Investing: How to
Revitalize Urban and Rural Communities With
Opportunity Funds.* JLW, 2020.

PRINCIPLE SEVEN:

https://uk.news.yahoo.com/10-quotes-john-mccain-
patriotism-002700837.html?guccounter=1&guce_
referrer=aHR0cHM6Ly93d3cuZ29vZ2xlLmN
vbS8&guce_referrer_sig=AQAAAE-3i2MtWMe
1zrdyjl3y86lk5d75b5FurSoFfFgWrph2o9nUczOTu-
OkHi9qMNx4Vk5EbRGJ2ShblWIsbCM_9rb2X-
SoGSn74gdzXSxWQWQv4JfED6X30K9KK81jBt-
nEgvPZRgr3lG6O0mcSuK5K1H2P9oNsTvFBu27-
IPrNezkn91k

https://www.vox.com/policy-and-politics/2018/8/25/
17782572/john-mccain-barack-obama-statement-
2008-video

https://www.nbcnews.com/politics/2020-election/
everything-trump-has-said-about-2020-field-insults-
all-n998556

https://www.liveabout.com/funny-one-liners-rodney-dangerfield-2832427

https://www.independent.co.uk/news/world/americas/us-politics/trump-insults-children-bully-us-school-racist-xenophobic-a9334911.html

https://time.com/5320865/maxine-waters-confront-trump-staffers-family-separation-policy/

https://www.npr.org/2019/04/23/716258113/kathy-griffin-life-after-the-trump-severed-head-controversy

https://www.pewresearch.org/fact-tank/2019/06/19/partisans-say-respect-and-compromise-are-important-in-politics-particularly-from-their-opponents/

http://sfppr.org/2016/08/president-ronald-reagans-use-of-humor/

https://www.washingtontimes.com/news/2019/oct/17/elijah-cummings-mourned-republicans-friend-statesm/

PRINCIPLE EIGHT:

http://www.citizensproject.org/2016/04/19/reclaiming-american-values/

https://abc7news.com/health/robert-kraft-uses-patriots-plane-to-deliver-n95-masks-from-china/6070730/

https://www.chicagotribune.com/lifestyles/sc-hate-has-no-home-here-posters-0201-20170202-story.html

https://www.cnn.com/2017/01/31/us/muslim-jewish-children-at-protest-irpt-trnd/index.html

PRINCIPLE NINE:

https://www.brainyquote.com/quotes/michael_bloomberg_450306

https://www.investopedia.com/updates/adam-smith-wealth-of-nations/

https://www.investopedia.com/terms/c/capitalism.asp

https://www.business-humanrights.org/en/dupont-lawsuits-re-pfoa-pollution-in-usa

https://www.thebalance.com/trump-plans-to-reduce-national-debt-4114401

https://hbswk.hbs.edu/item/can-health-care-companies-learn-to-compete

https://www.cnn.com/interactive/2020/03/politics/coronavirus-trump-cdc-timeline/

https://www.youtube.com/watch?v=ExWLn86Mu_g

https://apnews.com/f9fb8c41b7f8acc215e3ec78ca32210a

https://www.thebalance.com/how-outsourcing-jobs-affects-the-u-s-economy-3306279

https://www.usatoday.com/story/news/nation/
2020/04/07/who-dying-coronavirus-
more-black-people

PRINCIPLE TEN:

https://www.quotemaster.org/Compromise

https://www.realclearpolitics.com/articles/2012/
10/06/men_of_principle_and_the_lost_art_of_
compromise_115646.html

https://www.goodreads.com/quotes/7051258-an-
open-mind-is-not-an-empty-one

https://longtermrisk.org/files/possible-ways-to-
promote-compromise.pdf

EPILOGUE:

https://www.forbes.com/quotes/5423/

https://www.schulichleaders.com/best-thing-about-
future-it-comes-one-day-time

ABOUT THE AUTHOR:
JIM WHITE, PHD

Dr. Jim White is Chairman and CEO of Post Harvest Technologies, Inc. and Growers Ice Company, Inc., founder and CEO of PHT Opportunity Fund LP, and founder and president of JL White International, LLC.

He is the author of several acclaimed books—most recently, *Opportunity Investing: How to Revitalize Urban and Rural Communities with Opportunity Funds*. He is also author of the best-seller *What's My Purpose? A Journey of Personal and Professional Growth*. The book, which has been lauded by such industry leaders as Steven M.R. Covey and Jack Canfield, seeks to change readers by helping them to identify key truths while breaking down the main barriers (the Five Masks) to fulfillment.

Dr. White is also the founder of the customized year-long leadership and management transformation process, The Circle of Success; Jim White's Classic Movie Series; and The Red Carpet Tour. These innovative events have attracted more than 100,000 participants worldwide, including Fortune 500 CEOs, management teams, entrepreneurs, governments, and trade associations.

He first found his entrepreneurial spirit at age five when he created his first business—collecting and selling Coke bottles to help support his family. From these humble beginnings, Jim went on to serve his country in Vietnam before entering the corporate world upon his return. Along the way, he would go from high school dropout to academic triumph, eventually earning a B.S. in Civil Engineering, an MBA, and a Ph.D. in Psychology and Organizational Behavior.

Dr. White achieved international recognition as CEO of Blount World Trade Corporation; owner and Managing Director of ACEC Centrifugal Pumps NV, Belgium; and as Vice-President and Division Manager of Ingersoll Rand Equipment Corporation.

Throughout his career, he has bought, expanded, and sold 23 companies, operating in 44 countries. He acquires struggling businesses to revive and develop them into profitable enterprises using his business turnaround strategy. To date, Dr. White has generated more than $1.8 billion in revenue.